Cambridge Elements

Elements in Indigenous Environmental Research

Series Editors
Dina Gilio-Whitaker
California State University San Marcos
Clint Carroll
University of Colorado Boulder
Joy Porter
University of Birmingham
Associate Editor
Matthias Wong
National University of Singapore

DEFENDING COMMUNITY, TERRITORY, AND INDIGENOUS ENVIRONMENTAL RELATIONS

Levi Gahman
University of Liverpool

Filiberto Penados
Galen University

Cristina Coc
Maya Leaders Alliance

Shelda-Jane Smith
University of Liverpool

CAMBRIDGE
UNIVERSITY PRESS

Shaftesbury Road, Cambridge CB2 8EA, United Kingdom

One Liberty Plaza, 20th Floor, New York, NY 10006, USA

477 Williamstown Road, Port Melbourne, VIC 3207, Australia

314–321, 3rd Floor, Plot 3, Splendor Forum, Jasola District Centre,
New Delhi – 110025, India

103 Penang Road, #05–06/07, Visioncrest Commercial, Singapore 238467

Cambridge University Press is part of Cambridge University Press & Assessment,
a department of the University of Cambridge.

We share the University's mission to contribute to society through the pursuit of
education, learning and research at the highest international levels of excellence.

www.cambridge.org
Information on this title: www.cambridge.org/9781009454544

DOI: 10.1017/9781009454599

First published 2025

A catalogue record for this publication is available from the British Library

ISBN 978-1-009-45454-4 Hardback
ISBN 978-1-009-45457-5 Paperback
ISSN 2755-0826 (online)
ISSN 2755-0818 (print)

Cambridge University Press & Assessment has no responsibility for the persistence
or accuracy of URLs for external or third-party internet websites referred to in this
publication and does not guarantee that any content on such websites is, or will remain,
accurate or appropriate.

For EU product safety concerns, contact us at Calle de José Abascal, 56, 1°, 28003
Madrid, Spain, or email eugpsr@cambridge.org

Defending Community, Territory, and Indigenous Environmental Relations

Elements in Indigenous Environmental Research

DOI: 10.1017/9781009454599
First published online: August 2025

Levi Gahman
University of Liverpool

Filiberto Penados
Galen University

Cristina Coc
Maya Leaders Alliance

Shelda-Jane Smith
University of Liverpool

Author for correspondence: Filiberto Penados, fpenados@galen.edu.bz

Abstract: This Element addresses a range of pressing challenges and crises by introducing readers to the Maya struggle for land and self-determination in Belize, a former British colony situated in the Caribbean and Central America. In addition to foregrounding environmental relations, the text provides deeper understandings of Q'eqchi' and Mopan Maya people's dynamic conceptions and collective defence of community and territory. To do so, the authors centre the voices, worldviews, and experiences of Maya leaders, youth, and organisers who are engaged in frontline resistance and mobilisations against institutionalised racism and contemporary forms of dispossession. Broadly, the Element offers an example of how Indigenous communities are reckoning with the legacies of empire whilst confronting the structural violence and threats to land and life posed by the driving forces of capital accumulation, neoliberal development, and coloniality of the state. Ultimately, this Element illustrates the realities, repercussions, and transformative potential of grassroots movement-building 'from below'. This title is also available as open access on Cambridge Core.

Keywords: self-determination, environmental defence, Indigenous land rights, colonialism, resistance

ISBNs: 9781009454544 (HB), 9781009454575 (PB), 9781009454599 (OC)
ISSNs: 2755-0826 (online), 2755-0818 (print)

Contents

1 Introduction, Methodology, and Conceptual Framework

Participatory Research and Respecting Indigenous Epistemologies

This Element provides an in-depth exploration of the Maya people's struggle for land and self-determination in southern Belize (see Figure 1). In so doing, we detail the ways in which rural Q'eqchi' and Mopan communities are defending territory and relations by confronting the historical legacies of colonialism and contemporary machinations of neoliberal development. Through participatory methods, creative expression, and culturally sensitive ways of co-producing movement-relevant research, the text serves as collaborative intervention that at once expands conventional academic scholarship, advocates for responsible, ethics-driven research, and promotes emancipatory praxis 'from below'.

Markedly, we steadfastly believe that the knowledges generated by liberatory social movements and Indigenous communities-in-struggle deserve equal recognition and carry just as much weight, if not more, as those offered by credentialed academics in bourgeois universities. On this point and as we write, our hearts remain with the people of Palestine. Another explicit twofold aim we maintain is to foster international solidarity and raise critical awareness about the environmental relations and political agency of the Maya participants, activists, elders, and youth who contributed and continue to inform our research. The eclectic sections that follow thus offer a vibrant illustration of the grounded realities and grassroots mobilisations of Maya leaders and land defenders who are challenging structural inequality, institutionalised racism, and extinction narratives about Indigenous people, all of which persist across the Caribbean and Central America.

Regarding methodology, in the spirit of respecting 'otherwise worlds' and valuing *rooted* Indigenous epistemologies, this Element emerged out of ongoing participatory research that has been led and co-designed by Maya activists and collaborators from southern Belize. The iterative process (as opposed to a short-term, one-off project) has spanned nearly ten years and continues to involve annual undertakings that employ creative methods as a means of documenting and amplifying the 'joys, pains, and dreams' – as well as the environmental relations – of Maya communities. Activities have included Maya-developed arts-based dreaming exercises, photovoice exhibitions, transverse walks, heritage site go-along interviews, envisioning sessions, team-based ethno-mapping, interactive games, collective reflection circles, intergenerational focus groups, participatory film-making, and youth media training.

In consulting Maya community members and taking stock of the material we gathered throughout the entire research and outreach process, we have intentionally opted for a mosaic structure that offers readers a bricolage-esque series of unorthodox yet accessible sections. These are composed of and include critical academic

Figure 1 *Ch'och*, the lands the Maya people belong to, care for, and defend.
Credit: Roberto Kus, Maya Leaders Alliance

analyses sourced from scholarship; edited question-and-answer transcriptions of dialogue circles; composite first-person summaries of in-depth activist interviews; a photo essay foregrounding the perspectives of Maya youth; author and informant narrative reflections; and a series of images interspersed throughout the text that enlivens the prose via vivid snapshots of day-to-day Maya realities.[1]

This approach was selected because we believe it not only enriches the reading experience but also evokes and engenders how researchers can respect and remain beholden to the diverse epistemological methods, terms, and preferences of Indigenous contributors. Bringing the kaleidoscopic sections together and putting them into conversation with one another is further generative because it provides a more holistic view of the Maya people's pluralistic pursuit of self-determination by highlighting the connections that exist between their environmental stewardship, cultural heritage, and political struggle, which are not uncommon to Indigenous groups all over the world. In short, we feel the integration of the variegating sections found throughout this Element will deepen understandings of prismatic Indigenous knowledges, forms of resistance, and expressions of collectivity.

---

[1] Sections 2, 5, and 8 respectively include limited or revised content from these previously published articles: Penados, Gahman, and Smith (2022); Miss, Kus, Penados, and Gahman (2021); Toledo Anonymous Collective et al. (2022).

Academic Writing, Accountability, and the Politics of Representation

Crucially, the composition and content of this Element have involved and been informed by several Indigenous activists, movement organisers, and Maya leaders. In stating this, we want to offer an important caveat about the politics of accountability, collective writing, and representation. Kindly note that the text, while crafted with care, reverence, and introspection, neither fully incorporates nor definitively encapsulates the entire spectrum of diverse opinions, standpoints, and preferences regarding tone, tenor, and critical analyses that constitute the pluralistic Maya communities. Despite substantive guidance and review by select Maya collaborators and local authorities, it is admittedly impossible to fully capture either the intricacies or totality of the various perspectives and realities that exist across all the Maya villages and organisations of southern Belize.

Relatedly, we remain assiduously aware of the inescapable and exploitative power dynamics inherent in conducting research with Indigenous communities (Tuck, 2009). We have attempted to address these politically charged and imperfect dynamics head-on through self-reflexive practice, collaborative dialogue, and cyclical consent processes. Further, by granting contributors control over their narratives and integrating feedback from informants and knowledge holders recurrently, we have endeavoured to attenuate the tensions that exist between the insularity of hyper-individualistic Eurocentric knowledge production (Cupples and Grosfuguel, 2019) and collectivity of Indigenous epistemologies as diligently, responsibly, and transparently as possible. While the troubling complexities and fraught politics of co-producing academic research with social movements and Indigenous organisers can seemingly never be resolved fully within formal Western university settings (Smith, 2012), we have maintained our commitment to listening attentively, local ethical protocols, open consultation, and cultural humility throughout the process, and we have continued to acknowledge our fallibility and limitations.

With respect to author positionalities, Filiberto, a Yucatec Maya scholar-activist from Belize with a background in Indigenous methods who has supported Maya communities across Toledo District for more than two decades, was initially authorised to facilitate research years ago. Similarly, Cristina, a Q'eqchi' Maya activist and mother from the village of Laguna, has been deeply engaged in grassroots organising, land defence, and extra-academic community-based research for nearly twenty years. Levi, a non-Indigenous researcher who has focused on militant struggles for self-determination 'from below' in Central American, Caribbean, and occupied Palestinian contexts for fifteen years, began contributing in 2015 and has been working with the movement ever since. Later, in 2019, Shelda, a non-Indigenous researcher of Caribbean descent from Liverpool who specialises in critical health studies, joined the team. Upon respectively coming aboard, Levi and Shelda, as non-Indigenous collaborators, were and continue to be trained in and adhere to the evolving cultural safety protocols of the Maya villages. Trust, rapport, and reciprocity thereby continue to be galvanised through mutual respect, comradely relations, and long-term commitment – not to mention lasting convivial friendships.

Regarding the Maya voices found throughout the text, it is paramount to realise there is always a risk that certain participant quotes or excerpts might be misinterpreted, taken out of context, abstracted from analytical framing, or misconstrued in bad faith to distort and undermine Maya communities and their struggle. This point is especially germane to a work of this nature given the intense scrutiny Indigenous people and movements are subjected to globally, particularly when they are engaged in grassroots resistance and protracted conflicts with the state. Accordingly, any errors, omissions, provocations, or antagonisms within these pages are solely the responsibility of the academic authors and should neither be viewed nor used as reductive stereotypes of the heterogeneous Maya communities in question. As authors, we are opposed to the homogenising oversimplifications (and smear campaigns) that have historically been levied against multifaceted Indigenous movements that are committed to self-determination and defending the environment, as well as continue to be subjected to untold violence. With these requisite caveats in mind, an outline of the sections that follow is provided next.

Element Outline and Preview of the Ensuing Sections

To begin, the remaining part of Section 1 sets the conceptual stage by providing readers a glimpse of the realities being experienced by various Indigenous groups and environmental defenders across the world – whose lands and livelihoods are being threatened by deadly 'development' projects and dispossessive 'economic growth' agendas. We contend these fatal couplings are inextricably linked to the undying afterlives of empire. Section 2 introduces the Maya notions of *aj ral ch'och'* (being 'children of the Earth') and *se' komonil* (oneness-unity-harmony), which animate their community relations, cultural practices, and broader struggle, before shifting focus to the historical context of their legal cases, particularly a groundbreaking Caribbean Court of Justice (CCJ) land rights victory in 2015. This section also demonstrates how state power, race, and postcolonial nationalism are deployed to repress Indigenous people.

In Section 3, we foreground the voices of several *alcalde*s – that is, traditional elected village leaders – who are central to Maya customary governance and community cohesion. Headings throughout relate to answers *alcalde*s provided to questions we presented them about the external and internal challenges they face. Section 4, an interview with Maya organiser and co-author Cristina Coc, brings necessary attention to the pivotal roles played by Maya women, who are instrumental in reproducing, sustaining, and defending Maya communities, culture, and lifeways. The conversation details how Indigenous women simultaneously navigate multifarious forms of (patriarchal) oppression while fortifying community relations and pursuing their own dreams and aspirations.

The perspectives of Maya youth are featured in Section 5 via a photovoice essay that was one outcome of our shared and ongoing 'desire-based' research agenda. It focuses on young people's views of land, health, and nature, before ending with a joint reflection on joy and the future. Next, Section 6, an interview with Pablo Mis, a long-time Maya organiser, connects the climate crisis that Indigenous people are disproportionately experiencing to historical injustices owed to colonialism. Content here stresses the immediacy of recognising both Indigenous knowledges and land rights as effective forms of climate action, as well as serves as a bridge to Section 7, which critically examines the complex politics, colonial moorings, and useful – yet limited and paradoxical – potential of the Free Prior and Informed Consent (FPIC) protocol.

Section 8 explores both the personal and collective toll taken by environmental defence and frontline resistance. The contrasting parts detail the sacrifices made, courage required, and specific challenges faced by Maya activists and villagers who have taken a stand against land grabs, racist nationalism, colonial respectability politics, 'fortress conservation', and even the British royals. Our goal here is to underscore the ways in which grassroots collective action and care-driven mutuality serve as the lifeblood of the Maya people's fight for freedom and justice. Lastly, Section 9, via reflective prose, poetry, and rhizomatic links to decolonial literature, portrays the Maya pursuit of self-determination as a significant aspect of a historical–global struggle for sustainable and just futures not only for the Maya – but for all.

Struggles for Land and Life: The Dangers of Environmental Defence

Despite countless threats, resisting dispossession and protecting territory has been practised by Indigenous communities for centuries. Indeed, safeguarding land is nothing new for Indigenous people, but soberingly, being an environmental defender remains one of the deadliest vocations in the world. At present, they are the most at-risk demographic given they represent nearly one third of environmental activists killed worldwide (Le Billon and Lujala, 2020). In order to situate the Maya struggle for land and self-determination in the wider (post)colonial realities faced by Indigenous people globally, this subsection illustrates the violence at hand vis-à-vis 'development' and environmental defence (see Figure 2).

Historically, Indigenous people were amongst the first to be targeted by the brutal *terra nullius* ('empty lands') doctrine of empire and colonialism's exploitative notions of 'development' (Benton and Straumann, 2010). This is in addition to the invention and weaponisation of race they were subjected to as a means of dehumanising, condemning, and eliminating their communities and cultures (Fanon, 1963). Subsequently, and for generations, Indigenous land defenders have been exposed to predatory state-sponsored land grabs and the hostile logics of capital, yet they continue to lead the way in confronting development and collective resistance. For many Indigenous people, who are by no means monolithic, environmental protection goes beyond mainstream, statist understandings of the term.

Indigenous relationships with land and local ecosystems are typically rooted in connections to territory, which include material and spiritual dimensions, as

Figure 2 An *ab'ink* (community assembly) of local mappers discussing auto-delimitation between neighbouring villages, a critical aspect of protecting territory and Maya self-determination.

Credit: Roberto Kus, Maya Leaders Alliance

well as the interdependence that exists amongst humans, more-than-human life, and the natural world (Tynan, 2021). This means defending the environment is not relegated merely to conserving forests and curbing pollution, but also comprises preserving relations, sacred spaces, ancestral memories, and land-based practices that define their pluralistic worldviews and cultures. These integrated lifeways inherently position Indigenous communities as environmental defenders, particularly with respect to how many of their customs and *cosmovisións* challenge prevailing colonial–capitalist ideologies. In turn, land defenders face fierce repression from authoritarian governments and powerful business interests (McGrane, Mohamed, and Gahman, 2023).

In addition to abduction, disappearance, and murder, frontline activists experience slander, smear campaigns, sexual assault, criminalisation, and incarceration. Such forms of violence, which often unfold in remote hinterlands where rural communities depend on land for sustenance, are sanctioned and meted out by state officials, military personnel, transnational corporations, and private security forces (Menton and Le Billon, 2021). One major reason violence against land defenders is so prevalent is due to a lack of political will and accountability on the part of governments. Many countries either actively criminalise with impunity or purposefully fail to provide adequate legal protection to activists, leaving them vulnerable to attack, imprisonment, and even assassination (Global Witness, 2020). Additionally, corruption and collusion amongst state officials, ruling elites, and multinational corporations frequently exacerbate distress, injury, and trauma because advocates who attempt to report violations are routinely met with indifference, if not retribution.

Tragically, there has been a marked increase in the number of environmental defender murders around the world, with many cases never seeing killers brought to justice (McGee and Pettit, 2020). This leaves those affected devastated, fear-stricken, and traumatised, as well as affords victims no sense of closure, redress, or safety. Intimidation and harassment are also common as environmental defenders are regularly stalked, threatened, and surveilled online and offline. In addition, they experience myriad forms of physical violence, with some being abducted, beaten, tortured, and disappeared. Such reprisals are used to silence and discourage others from speaking out and taking a stand given the chilling effect such threats and assaults come with (Braaten, 2022).

To fully comprehend what lies at the roots and provokes environmental defence, it is essential to recognise the links conventional notions of 'development' have to colonialism and neoliberal modes of capital accumulation (Motta and Nilsen, 2011). As argued by Indigenous movements across the globe, for more than 500 years, imperial power and profit motives have disordered the world and created inequalities via exploitation and domination (EZLN, 2015).

These processes persist and are rationalised and perpetuated through discourses of 'national security' and 'economic development', which facilitate the enclosure and privatisation of what otherwise would be communal lands and 'the commons'. Gaining mineral rights, obtaining mining concessions, expropriating arable land, industrial logging of dense forests, and hyper-exploiting 'others' on plantations have regrettably become hallmarks of 'free trade', 'opening new markets', and 'stimulating growth'. Put succinctly, corporate entities and agents of empire both old and new continue to plunder the earth.

Notably, extractive agendas like these are disproportionately afflicting negatively racialised communities and women in the Global South (Tran et al., 2020). In many ways, dispossessive processes like this seem to be the banal status quo, often go unnoticed, and sometimes even appear to be 'slow', which we expand upon in the next subsection. Development aggression of this nature, however, is not going uncontested due to the grounded efforts and sacrifices being made by environmental defenders. Consequently, the forms of retaliatory violence and lethal force detailed earlier in this section are tangible realities Indigenous activists routinely must traverse.

Slow Violence, Colonial Histories, and Grassroots Resistance

Land defence has been a pillar of grassroots resistance for generations and continues to be an indispensable part of a growing global justice movement. The historical trajectories of colonialism, the reach of contemporary neoliberal development, and the failures of state-led environmental protection policies across numerous borders have left countless ecosystems endangered, with Indigenous communities remaining particularly vulnerable (Ghazoul and Kleinschroth, 2018). Environmental defenders are left to fight alone against powerful, well-funded corporate, government, and military actors that are heavily steeped in cultures of unsustainable growth, overconsumption, and waste. This has given rise to more awareness of 'slow violence' (Nixon, 2011), a form of systemic harm that unfolds gradually, often escaping immediate attention due to its seemingly subtle and incremental effects.

The concept of slow violence, which we feel is especially germane to the Maya struggle in southern Belize, encompasses a range of phenomena that cumulatively result in devastating impacts to individuals, communities, and ecologies. As a modality of structural violence, which is harm and exposure to premature death resulting from social systems that perpetuate inequality and limit access to resources (Farmer, 2004), slow violence represents the ways in which environmental debilitation, contamination, and dispossession occur over long stretches of time. Unlike wanton acts of lurid violence that capture oft-sensationalist media attention, slow violence is the ostensibly imperceptible and insidious attrition of community well-being and ecological health.

Examples of slow violence include the gradual deterioration of ecosystems and human vitality due to mining, pollution, deforestation, carbon release, and bio-magnification, as well as chronic exposure to carcinogens, toxins, and noxious pollutants, which disproportionately affect negatively racialised and low-income communities (Liboiron, 2021). In this vein, extractive capitalism's 'externalities', 'sacrifice zones', and 'profane spaces' (Losurdo, 2014) are grim examples of the slow violence associated with environmental injustice and institutionalised racism. For example, British, French, and Dutch colonial policies across the Caribbean, along with edicts from the Spanish Empire throughout Latin America, resulted in deforestation, erosion, nutrient loss, and increases in cancerous diseases because of enslavement, indentureship, and the industrialised plantation system (Beckford, 1972; Davis et al., 2019). By casting critical light on the covert processes that inflict ecological and social deterioration both spatially and temporally, slow violence underscores the importance of exposing and addressing 'common-sense' development and growth agendas.

Usefully, the notion of slow violence challenges conventional understandings of socio-environmental destruction by highlighting how the interlocking and long-term repercussions of various forms of structural violence and racial inequality play out across different contexts and places (Cahill and Pain, 2019). Discursively, then, slow violence can be employed as a heuristic tool to better describe how marginalised groups are exposed to persistent forms of colonial harm, abandonment, and alienation. At present, these deleterious trends are only accelerating for communities that rely on both marine and terrestrial ecosystems for their livelihoods, cultural heritage, and spiritual practices, including the Maya in southern Belize (Penados, Gahman, and Smith, 2022).

Unfortunately, the slow violence faced by Indigenous communities repeatedly fails to capture mainstream attention and generally goes unaddressed in both policy and practice. As a response, a growing assemblage of globally dispersed environmental defenders from diverse ethnic backgrounds is continuing to confront and resist the violence of development. Many are Indigenous community organisers who are challenging the profit-driven 'pro-growth' logics and ecologically destructive 'free trade' agreements that governments, international financial institutions, and multilateral organisations are failing – and refusing – to oppose (Zeng, Twang, and Carrasco, 2022).

Grassroots movements are diverse in composition and form, ranging from small collectives to (inter)national networks, and employ a wide array of protest strategies and repertoires. Tactics range from militant blockades and covert sabotage to mutual aid, awareness-raising campaigns, and legal action to mitigate damage being done to vulnerable communities and ecosystems (Gahman, Penados, and Smith, 2023). On this front, Indigenous environmental defenders are no stranger to direct action in the face of neoliberal 'business as usual' (Altamirano-Jimenez, 2013). Ironically, however, despite the fact that the United Nations (UN) and Intergovernmental Panel on Climate Change (IPCC) now recognise the crucial role Indigenous people and local knowledges play regarding effective climate action (IPCC, 2022), both human rights accords and multilateral institutions continue to fall short of enforcing policies that adequately protect Indigenous land defenders.

In linking the realities of environmental defence, slow violence, and colonial histories to the Maya communities of southern Belize, it is important to mention that whilst we as authors intentionally use and feel the descriptor 'environmental defender' is qualitatively accurate in light of the risks Maya organisers are taking to protect territory, community, and relations, the vast majority of contributors featured throughout this text do not explicitly self-identify as 'environmental defenders'. Our deliberate use of the term is not meant to impose upon them a fixed label, but rather is a rhetorical signifier we use due to the political connotations that come with the term 'environmental defender'. For us, the moniker accurately and evocatively captures the hostile conditions and imminent danger they, as Indigenous activists, experience as a result of their frontline efforts and grassroots praxis.

2 The Maya Struggle for Land, Life, and Self-Determination

History and Context: Race and Maya Realities in Southern Belize

Belize is part of Maya ancestral territory and emerged as a modern nation state in the colonial crucible where British and Spanish imperial forces and functionaries dispossessed, displaced, and deterritorialised Maya communities, as well as violently deracinated and imported enslaved African people and indentured South Asian groups, amongst others (Shoman, 1994) (see Figure 3). Through colonial penetration and administrative power, geographies and populations across the circum-Caribbean were fractured and reconfigured through the drafting of maps, imposition of arbitrary borders, and mobilisation of race, which often splintered Indigenous, arrivant, and involuntary settler communities (Bolland, 2003). Today, Belize is a multi-ethnic society and home to a diversity of demographic profiles, including three Maya linguistic groups: the Q'eqchi', Mopan, and Yucatec. The first two, the Q'eqchi' and Mopan, reside predominantly in southern Belize, primarily Toledo District, which is home to a total of forty-one Maya communities.

Figure 3 The temples of Lubaantun in Toledo District, Belize, a prominent reminder of how Maya history, heritage, and ancestral memory are rooted in and connected to land.

Credit: Roberto Kus, Maya Leaders Alliance

Within the Caribbean, matters and tensions related to race, indigeneity, and nationalism are complex and must be approached both critically and carefully given the region's experiences of Euro-American colonial domination, anti-Black, and anti-Indigenous racism, plural creolisations, and differential degrees of independence (Cordis, 2019; Jackson, 2012). Jackson (2014), in writing about the intricacies and internal conflicts that emerge at the nexus of race and the historical trajectories of enslavement, indentureship, and statist claims to political legitimacy in the Caribbean, argues that appeals to 'rightful owner-ship' of the postcolonial nation state as a result of having 'built the colony' through (coercive and captive) labour are fraught and ultimately reproduce colonial institutions and Eurocentric worldviews.

In analysing indigeneity, anti-Blackness, and postcolonial social relations in Guyana, which we feel are applicable to other geographies across the circum-Caribbean like Belize, Jackson (2014) offers prescient insight into the insepar-ability of anti-Black and anti-Indigenous racism – as well as how possibilities for reconciling incommensurate struggles for self-determination remain – when she writes:

> [A]nti-Blackness cannot be understood apart from the subordination of
> Indigenous peoples in early Empire, under colonialism, and ultimately in

> postcolonial nationalism throughout the Caribbean. Most writers and theorists tell us that Blacks had to be brought into the Caribbean because its Indigenous peoples disappeared or were too weak to work on plantations. This uncritical argument, that the disappearance of Indigenous peoples was the reason for the introduction of Black, and later indentured labor, hinders us from seeing how these two causalities are in fact irrevocably yoked. … We must reject the mystification of Indigenous relationships to land and recognize the complex and evolving, pre-colonial social and political systems that Indigenous peoples developed and which they seek to restore through claims for sovereignty and land rights.

Since both colonial contact and post-independent state-building in Belize, the Q'eqchi and Mopan Maya have been engaged in a prolonged fight to defend their ancestral territories, cultural heritage, and self-determined futures (Kus et al., 2023).[2] Traditionally, the Maya have held lands in common and derive individual rights of use from the community through collective processes of participatory consensus. Central to this communal and complex land tenure system are the *alcaldes*, an expression of Maya governance that existed prior to contact and has since been reconfigured several times over centuries via a dialectic between colonial power and Indigenous resistance (Mesh, 2017). The *alcaldes*, who are elected Maya community leaders internal to rural villages across southern Belize, facilitate the practice of direct democracy, conflict resolution, and community cohesion, as well as manage land use and boundary harmonisation processes (Penados, 2019).

For the past three decades, the *alcaldes* have been formally structured under an independent organisation known as the Toledo Alcaldes Association (TAA). The TAA is supported by the Maya Leaders Alliance (MLA), an autonomous coalition of grassroots Maya organisers who assist community members and are engaged in political advocacy and technical support (Gahman, Penados, and Greenidge, 2020). Markedly, an ethos of collectivity and economy of reciprocity lies at the heart of the Maya's social relations, practice of participatory governance, and relationships with ecosystems and heritage (Haines, 2012). For generations, and despite being targets of and struggling against empire, state authority, and capitalist development (Wainwright, 2011), the Maya have been able to maintain a certain degree of relative autonomy and retain their approaches to mutually stewarding, sharing, and enjoying communal lands, which is a departure from Western notions of claiming individual ownership over private property.

---

[2] A significant territorial dispute between Belize and Guatemala, which is rooted in colonial-era claims and tensions that persist despite diplomatic negotiations, still exists. The unresolved conflict is influential regarding regional geopolitics, but a detailed examination is admittedly beyond the scope of this focused Element. For a rich entry point, see Shoman (2018).

The latest iteration of territorial struggle and environmental defence emerged in the mid 1990s as a response to concessions granted without collective consent by the Belizean state to third-party multinational corporations to 'develop' (i.e. dispossess) Maya lands. Specifically, the government of Belize permitted logging concessions to Malaysian companies for timber extraction on nearly half a million acres of land traditionally used and occupied by Maya villagers (Anaya, 2008). Maya farmers only became aware of the concessions because they were confronted by loggers and heavy equipment in their backyards, a not altogether infrequent occurrence that is emblematic of racialised land-grabbing and extraction in the region (Loperena, 2022; Mollett, 2016).

Dispossession and State Power versus *Se' komonil* and *Aj ral ch'och'*

With respect to the struggle for land in Toledo District, it is vital to know that both the Belizean government and third-party extractive corporations (e.g. mining, logging, oil) have been responsible for a litany of documented violations of Free, Prior, and Informed Consent (FPIC) in the country (Penados et al., 2021). Essentially, that Maya people own, use, occupy, and depend upon traditional lands – and at the very least have a right to consultation and consent (i.e. FPIC) for anything that happens in their ancestral territories – has been ignored for decades (Campbell and Anaya, 2008). It is state-sponsored dispossession of this nature, which *presumably* would have been prevented by FPIC, that led to the Maya's most recent struggle for land and has included a protracted legal battle of more than twenty years.

During this time, Maya villagers and movement leaders have been forced into the courts at every level, which culminated in a watershed 2015 CCJ ruling that recognised their communal land rights (ELAW, 2015). In turn and at present, both smear campaigns and legal skirmishes continue, as does the Maya communities' fight for their relationships with territory and right to self-determination. Amidst the drawn-out and ongoing conflict, government administrators have routinely portrayed the Maya as primitive, unpatriotic, 'anti-development', and guilty of dismembering and 'Balkanising' Belize – that is, creating a state within a state – which is far from what the Maya have articulated as their goal. Contrariwise, at the centre of the Maya struggle is the aspiration to transform Belize into a country that would be more inclusive of and respectful towards Indigenous ways of being and social–environmental relations.

On this point, their struggle is not unlike that of the Zapatistas of southern Mexico, chiefly Maya themselves, who amidst their emancipatory uprising in 1994 and ensuing construction of autonomy asserted 'never again a Mexico without us' and have expressed a desire to build 'a world in which many worlds fit' (EZLN, 2015).[3] In the same spirit, for the Maya of southern Belize, as one contributor to the movement succinctly summarised, they are not seeking to secede from the nation or abolish the country, but rather hope to eventually reside in 'a Belize where many Belizeans fit'. Notably, throughout their struggle, numerous Maya organisers have emphasised that whilst entering both domestic and international courts is often necessary for tactical reasons related to Western notions of land rights, neither have any real bearing on or legitimacy when it comes to defining the *relationships* the Maya have with their ancestral territories, which they refer to as *se' komonil* (oneness) and *aj ral ch'och'* (being 'children of the Earth').

Se' komonil is a deeply layered term used by the Q'eqchi' Maya that refers to solidaristic, communal living. It implies a commitment to each other, to resolving conflict and seeking peace, harmony, and holistic health. In essence it is about living well together. *Se' komonil* is the heart of the collective essence of the Maya people and the lifeblood of their customary practices and reciprocal relationships not only with each other, but with the land, forests, rivers, waterways, ancestral territories, and the non-human world. *Se' komonil* is inextricably linked to community, socio-environmental relations, and the concept the Maya use to express their collective identity, *aj ral ch'och'*, which is how they define themselves as Indigenous people. *Aj ral ch'och'* is a Q'eqchi' term that approximately translates to being 'children of the Earth'. It is composed of the phrase *aj ral*, 'an offspring', and *ch'och'*, which represents the Earth, soil, and clay.

Ontologically, being *aj ral ch'och'* means maintaining a dynamic and symbiotic relationship with territory and each other. It encompasses human-ecological interdependence, a shared socio-territorial subjectivity, (bio)cultural heritage inextricably linked to local ecosystems, maintaining community environmental health, stewarding the commons, rooted foodways sourced from organic regenerative agroforestry, and the collective practice of spiritual ceremony. In short, *aj ral ch'och'* speaks to being from and living on the land – that is, belonging to it, depending on it, caring for it, and being *of* it. In this way, *se' komonil* and *aj ral ch'och'* resonate with other conceptions of 'good living' such

---

[3] The Zapatistas of Chiapas, Mexico, and the Maya communities in southern Belize also differ significantly in their tactics and strategies with respect to pursuing autonomy. While the Zapatista Army of National Liberation (EZLN) took up arms against the state in its revolutionary struggle for 'democracy, freedom, and justice', the Maya communities in Toledo District, Belize, have refrained from armed insurrection and have utilised strategic litigation and international law to assert their rights to land and self-determination. A point of comparison is the Zapatistas' *Sexta Declaración* (Sixth Declaration), which overtly calls for anti-capitalist resistance globally and contrasts with the more localised, legal avenues of the Maya in Belize. Markedly, both movements stress the necessity of grassroots organising and neither has called for the cessation of their respective national identities or countries.

Figure 4 A Maya fire ceremony being performed outdoors in a rural Maya village. The ceremony connects community members to the spiritual world, ancestors, land, and each other.

Credit: Roberto Kus, Maya Leaders Alliance

as *suma qamaña*, *suma kawsay*, and *buen vivir*, which are socio-territorially situated yet uniquely distinct and used by different Indigenous groups across South America in their respective contexts (Cuestas-Caza, 2018).

Ultimately, for the Maya communities of southern Belize, *aj ral ch'och'* is used to assert: 'We are both *from* and *of* this land.' As we will see in the subsections to come, state-sanctioned enclosure (Grandia, 2012), infrastructure projects (Haines, 2018), and land grabs continue to threaten Maya lands, customary governance, and the embodiment and practice of both *aj ral ch'och* and *se' komonil* (see Figure 4).

Strategic Litigation: Protracted Legal Battles and a 2015 CCJ Victory

While numerous leaders and activists from Maya communities fully recognise that neither statist legal systems nor top-down (inter)national policies are key drivers of social change and self-determination, the movement has been impelled to engage in strategic litigation against the government to formally secure legal land rights, which has been notoriously combative. The Maya filed their first lawsuit in the Supreme Court of Belize in 1996, which proved futile as the hearing was delayed for almost two years. Frustrated with the lack of response, in 1998, Maya communities again petitioned their case before the Inter-American Commission on Human Rights (IACHR, 2004), arguing:

> [T]he State has granted logging and oil concessions on the Maya lands *without meaningful consultations* with the Maya people and in a manner that has caused *substantial environmental harm and threatens long term and irreversible damage* to the natural environment upon which the Maya depend. (emphasis added)

After six years, the IACHR produced a report siding with the Maya people. It agreed that the Maya have collective rights to the lands they had been traditionally 'using, occupying, and enjoying' and that the government had violated Maya property rights by failing to recognise, delimit, demarcate, title, and protect the territory where those rights existed (IACHR, 2004). Additionally, the IACHR found the state was responsible for 'granting logging and oil concessions to third parties to utilize the property and resources ... in the absence of effective consultations with and the informed consent of the Maya people'. The IACHR recommended the government of Belize define, distinguish, and title Maya ancestral lands, a mandate that was largely ignored – and a process that continues to be frustrated to this day – by the state. While some of the permits were cancelled, the government refused to accept the Maya as rightful owners to ancestral lands and repudiated recognising their right to FPIC, consequently meaning there was and has been no subsequent delimitation, demarcation, or titling of Maya lands.

Between the Maya filing the initial claim in 1996 and the IACHR ruling of 2004, there had been several attempts at negotiation with the state prompted by the commission. One of the outcomes of these discussions was the 'Ten Points of Agreement', in which the government fleetingly acknowledged Maya rights to land (Wainwright, 2021). While this seemed like a major advance, it did not result in any meaningful action by the state. Responding to a lack of political will and progress by the government, the Maya made their way back into court in 2007. This time, however, instead of focusing on Maya territory in its entirety (at the time this would have encompassed thirty-nine Maya communities, but there are now forty-one), the legal team concentrated on two individual communities: Santa Cruz and Conejo.

In deliberations, the government of Belize shockingly argued that Maya people, while Indigenous, were not indigenous to Belize and consequently have no rights to land. The Supreme Court of Belize, on the contrary, ruled in favour of the Maya people, recognising them as indigenous to Belize and thus as having rights to land. The verdict issued by Chief Justice of Belize Judge Abdulai Conteh, averred that the expropriation of Indigenous territories, initially by the British and later by successive postcolonial administrations, did not negate Maya land claims. The court further ordered the government to 'respect and protect' Maya communal land rights and refrain from granting concessions without consultation and receiving informed consent from the communities (SCB, 2007).

After the ruling, the state adopted the position that the case only pertained to the two specified communities, Santa Cruz and Conejo. This meant that, in the eyes of the government, the other thirty-seven Maya communities of Toledo District had no rights to either land or the FPIC protocol. The remaining thirty-seven Maya communities, which were not included in the 2007 case, subsequently had to file for collective land rights in 2008. After two years, in 2010, the Supreme Court of Belize once again issued a decision in favour of the Maya villages. This ruling clarified that the judgment passed in 2007 was applicable to the entirety of Toledo District – that is, all thirty-nine Maya communities' collective land rights were to be respected. The Supreme Court also dispensed an injunction prohibiting any further state sponsored concessions based on the Maya's long-standing use and occupancy of lands across southern Belize (ELAW, 2015).

The Maya subsequently faced two appeals initiated by the government. The first took place in the Court of Appeal, with the second going to the CCJ – the highest court with jurisdiction in Belize. In 2013, the Court of Appeal upheld the lower court's 2010 ruling, and in 2015, the CCJ did the same via a consent order (Caserta, 2018). The decision rendered by the CCJ asserted that Maya villages hold title to their ancestral lands, which was also a legal recognition of Maya governance and customary law. The 2015 CCJ consent order – an unprecedented ruling in the Caribbean regarding the acknowledgement of Indigenous land rights by an international court – decrees that traditional Maya notions of communal landownership are equivalent to the Western–liberal conceptions of private property recognised in the Belizean constitution.

Backlash and Reprisal: Criminalising Maya Land-Heritage Defence

The Maya communities' victory, and wider legal and extrajudicial pursuit of self-determination under the shadow of Belize's Westminster-modelled state, has not gone without repercussion (see Figure 5).[4] The protracted and recurrent forms of direct repression and slow violence, in addition to the subsequent court battles that ensued because of state-sanctioned FPIC violations against the Maya, have coincided with intimidation, criminalisation, and smear campaigns

---

[4] We deliberately use the descriptor 'Westminster-modelled' given the necessary political work it does in explicitly signifying the coloniality of governance in Belize and numerous administrative institutions across the Caribbean.

Figure 5 Maya leaders gather to communicate the results of an *ab'ink* related to the government's attempt to unilaterally file an FPIC protocol without appropriate consultation.

Credit: Roberto Kus, Maya Leaders Alliance

(Toledo Anonymous Collective et al., 2022). From the first day of their struggle, Maya organisers have been accosted, harassed, threatened, and arbitrarily arrested via prejudicial mobilisations of racist nationalism by government officials (Penados, Gahman, and Smith, 2022).

For example, the Julian Cho Society (JCS), a non-governmental organisation (NGO) in Toledo District committed to advancing Indigenous land rights and culturally safe educational initiatives, emerged from the Maya's efforts to protect the environment. Established in the mid 2000s, the JCS is named after Julian Armando Cho, a Mopan Maya educator and human rights advocate who, in the 1990s, confronted corporate extractors and state complicity. Cho mobilised communities and led demonstrations against multinational logging companies that were unilaterally granted concessions by the government. Heartbreakingly, Cho was found lifeless outside his residence in December 1998 (Wainwright, 2011). His tragic passing conspicuously occurred amidst vocal protests he was directing against both the state and large business firms, as well as shortly after he received multiple threats related to his activism. While the circumstances surrounding his death remain ambiguous and contested, his legacy continues to influence and motivate the Maya to this day.

Another flashpoint incident of retaliatory criminalisation occurred in June 2015, when Cristina Coc, a Q'eqchi' activist and spokesperson of the MLA, was arrested along with twelve other Maya environmental defenders. Dubbed the 'Santa Cruz 13', the villagers were protecting a local heritage site at Uxbenká by preventing unsanctioned settlement upon sacred grounds. After asking for and being denied assistance by state authorities to halt the heritage destruction, the group were adjudicating the situation through the Maya customary governance system – the *alcalde*s. The situation was heated and complicated given the perpetrator, who threatened gun violence against village residents multiple times, was an Afrodescendant Kriol man (Baines and Zaragar, 2024). Even though the situation was handled by the *alcalde*s and village leaders, who are officially recognised as lower court magistrates and only intervened after requesting but being rebuffed by the state, the government used the incident as a pretext to arrest members of the village, paint the Maya as a 'violent mob', and stoke divisive Kriol–Maya (Black–Indigenous) race relations.

Shortly after and amidst the havoc-laden fallout, the significance and implications of the government's ill-advised arrests were highlighted by the United Nations Special Rapporteur on the Rights of Indigenous Peoples, Victoria Tauli-Corpuz, who, in an international statement, noted that the state's handling of the situation displayed blatant and 'troubling disregard' for Maya property rights. Tauli-Corpuz (OHCHR, 2015) went on to stress that – in the face of the government's benighted justification for jailing Coc and the Maya land defenders – the 'current situation of conflict and mistrust cannot be allowed to persist'. Tellingly, and not without taking an emotional, physical, and financial toll on Maya community members for months, after approximately a year of court appearances, prevarication, and vilification on the part of the state, the entire set of charges against the Santa Cruz 13, including Coc, were dropped. This story is neither anecdotal nor happenstance because the criminalisation, public denigration, and abduction of Indigenous environmental defenders continues to be a preferred method of numerous postcolonial governments across Latin American and the Caribbean (Guzmán Hormazábal, 2019).

Several points are worth highlighting here. Firstly, the government habitually failed to obtain consent from Maya people in granting concessions on Maya lands. Secondly, to correct this, the Maya were forced into multiple time-, energy-, and resource-consuming court proceedings that lasted nearly twenty years. Thirdly, the contentious and lengthy legal melee arose because the Maya's presence and use of their lands was either conveniently ignored or wholly irrelevant to the state. Lastly, the government of Belize brazenly and bizarrely called into question the Maya peoples' indigeneity by denying their ancestral presence and connections to land – that is, arguing that the Maya are not indigenous to Belize. Moreover, in issuing a verdict in favour of the Maya, the CCJ ordered the state to implement a meaningful consultation process related to the FPIC protocol and delimitation, demarcation, and titling of Maya lands based on their customary uses and notions of complex tenure. Since that time, numerous violations and legal clashes have ensued due to the state's obstinacy and disdain for the Maya communities, MLA, and TAA – the appellants of the 2015 CCJ case.

In sum, for decades, numerous Maya community members have attested to racial discrimination and being treated as 'uncivilised indians' by government officials. Likewise, when the Maya have asserted themselves as Indigenous people, the response of the state has been to disparage and cast doubt on their indigeneity by relying on earlier colonial violence and dispossession to argue Maya land rights have been extinguished. Additionally, when a collective standpoint has been expressed through traditional Maya leadership, the *alcalde*s, the Belizean government has denied and rebuked their legitimacy, not only calling into question customary governance but deputising itself as the arbiter of who should be recognised as a Maya representative and how consultation with Maya communities must be structured. As we will see in Section 3, the Maya communities, in particular the *alcalde*s, continue to resist the racist nationalism of the Westminster-modelled state.

3 The Voice of the *Alcalde*s: A Dialogue on Maya Struggle

This section focuses on traditional Maya leadership, the alcaldes, *and their perspectives of the Maya struggle in two parts. The first half offers a historical overview of the* alcalde *system in Belize, with the second featuring Maya voices sourced from dialogue and reflection sessions with local leaders. Via thematic answers and direct quotes that appear under question headings, the* alcaldes *share their experiences and viewpoints on land, the nature of village leadership, and their aspirations amidst state-sanctioned efforts to domesticate, discipline, and disappear an evolving governance system that is central to Maya self-determination.*

A Brief Genealogy and Overview of the Maya *Alcalde*s of Belize

The traditional leadership and governance system among the Maya in southern Belize is today referred to as the *alcalde* system (Mesh, 2017) (see Figure 6). While rooted in and retaining many long-standing aspects of Maya customary governance, both its contemporary name and form are partially the product of competing empires attempting to bring the Maya under Spanish and later British control. At present, the *alcalde* system remains a political terrain of struggle and

Figure 6 Members of the TAA pause for spiritual reflection during *Qa'xtasink K'anjel*, the handing over of leadership duties and collective work from one group of *alcalde*s to the next.

Credit: Roberto Kus, Maya Leaders Alliance

site of contestation that lays bare the violence of the state and showcases the resistance and resilience of the Maya people (Penados, 2019).

The term *alcalde*, which translates to 'minor judge' or 'mayor', was brought to Mesoamerica by Spanish conquistadors and later used by British imperialists.[5] It was implemented as part of broader political project of installing administrative figures who would rule over the Maya and co-opt existing local leaders to facilitate indirect rule. Amidst this colonial cauldron, and for centuries, the Maya have creatively found ways to sustain and practise relative degrees of autonomous governance through the *alcalde* system. This is due to their opposition to colonial domination, as well as geographical proximity – that is, being primarily located in the mountainous hinterlands and remote forests of rural southern Belize (Wainwright, 2011). Significantly, the *alcalde*s remain a critical element and ever-evolving institution of Indigenous leadership.

As traditional leaders, *alcalde*s are beholden to long-standing customary Maya law and are known as the *Jolomil kaleb'aal/Polil ka*, meaning 'the one who leads on the path', in addition to being 'the eyes, ears, and mouth of the

---

[5] The term *alcalde* also translates and is used to refer to 'mayors' in Latin America. In the Maya context of southern Belize, the administrative role village *alcalde*s play is related to (Indigenous) customary laws and practices.

community'. The latter expression is noteworthy because, unlike partisan politicians and state ministries, *alcaldes* cannot issue decisions unless processes of direct democracy have been followed. That is, *alcaldes* represent and act on behalf of the community's voice, but only do so after communal deliberation takes place at participatory village meetings. In the *alcalde* system, the maximum authority is the community assembly, known as the *ab'ink*, a Q'eqchi' term that translates 'to listen'. *Alcaldes* can thus be recalled relatively swiftly if a collective mandate is misrepresented or goes unaddressed.

At the level of individual communities, each elects an *alcalde*, a deputy *alcalde*, and three to seven assistants (referred to as village police) depending on village size. The *alcalde* is a community's central representative and responsible for maintaining peace, organising collective work, resolving conflicts, and overseeing the customary land tenure system. Village police correspondingly act as messengers and stewards of the community. They also assist *alcaldes* in enforcing laws, but, as the *alcaldes* we spoke to clarified, are politically distinct and unlike government-sanctioned police forces, which they viewed as far more adversarial, intimidatory, and punitive.

In a complex dual role that combines Maya customary governance with state authority, *alcaldes*, upon being elected by the community, are also sworn in by Belize's attorney general. From a statutory perspective, the role is managed under the Inferior Courts Act, which limits an *alcalde*'s function to lower court magistrate. Since independence in 1981, the government has consistently viewed the *alcaldes* as 'backward', 'outmoded', and an 'obstacle' to 'modern' development. The state has further sought to diminish the authority of the *alcaldes* and replace them with state-based village councils, which remain intact and can create internal tensions and community conflicts. From a Maya standpoint, being an *alcalde* is a time-honoured responsibility and leadership role that sustains customary law and practice, which is a vital aspect of Indigenous self-determination and ultimately what is at stake.

Current Challenges and Threats faced by the *Alcaldes* and TAA

One of the most important innovations in Maya governance is the aforementioned TAA, which the Maya established in the 1980s as an autonomous association and vehicle for organising across communities and collective advocacy. All Maya villages elect *alcaldes* every two years, who compose the TAA. This regional body functions as a space for dialogue, joint planning, and concerted action on issues that affect the Maya beyond individual communities. The association is a mechanism for resolving inter-village conflicts but has no jurisdiction over any respective community. In this way, the TAA serves as an intergenerational knowledge-bearing body and custodian of customary practices. It facilitates *alcalde* elections, offers advice, and assists in resolving conflicts and grievances. Upon request, the TAA also provides technical support to communities when they engage with government ministries and/or third parties, which is particularly pivotal on matters related to development, consultation, and FPIC.

Overall, the critical function of the *alcalde* system, and in particular the TAA, continues to be its role as a catalyst and means of *collective* organising, advocacy, and representation. *Alcalde*s are democratically nominated and elected through customary practice, meaning no one campaigns for the position given they are selected on the strength of their character, humility, experience, and trajectory in the traditional leadership system. Historically, they tend to be men with little formal education but with vast knowledge of customary Maya law and they are well respected in their communities. More recently, there have been increasing efforts to remove the barriers women face regarding pathways into leadership, and, importantly, there are now a handful of women *alcalde*s. In terms of governance and decision-making, *alcalde*s operate outside networks of political patronage and clientelism, as well as represent a unified Indigenous institution, the TAA, which makes them a target of the state.

In recent years, particularly after the 2015 CCJ ruling, the government has escalated attacks on the *alcalde*s (especially the TAA) given their role in the land rights movement and because the TAA is a point source of solidarity across Maya villages. It has done so through slander, defamation, attempted bribes, and 'lawfare' – that is, legal challenges aimed at discrediting and disavowing the *alcalde*s and TAA, all of which continue. On this point, *alcalde*s are frequently denigrated for their perceived lack of education, as well as regularly viewed as 'pawns and puppets' of external actors (e.g. political parties, businesses, churches) who are incapable of building and contributing to a grassroots movement that is challenging the state. Amidst these historical–contemporary complexities, it is paramount to realise that the *alcalde*s and TAA remain pillars of customary governance and unity, not to mention they are also key actors at the centre of the Maya struggle.

Considering all of this, and as a way to ensure that *alcalde*s' voices are heard, two authors, Filiberto and Levi, interviewed seven past presidents and vice presidents of the TAA and four younger MLA staff members to document their understandings of leadership and the challenges they face with respect to self-determination and state power. In keeping with the collective consensus-building practices of the *alcalde* system and participant preferences, their statements were integrated into a single multi-part compilation, which is presented next. The content was later presented to all interviewees in its entirety for their review, approval, and consent. Each paragraph represents anonymised individual responses to questions we posed, which can be seen in the subsection headings and which are followed in some instances by thematic answers.

Question: What led to the formation and resilience of the TAA?

The TAA was established in the 1980s. There were only a few students going to high school in our community, and we thought that if the government provided a bus, more students could attend. A community member wrote a letter and went to the Ministry of Education, but they asked, 'Who are you?' We then asked the village *alcalde* to sign, and we went again, but no progress. So we got more villages involved and their *alcalde*s signed. Out of this, we formed an *alcalde*s' committee. Other communities wanted to do the same, so they joined, and we grew and became the *alcalde*s' association.

In those days, when we were organising, we paid our own passage or we walked to visit communities. We agreed that we had to go to the people. It is not about people coming to your office. We cannot be like the government where people have to go to Belmopan. Our success was going to the people because there they started to participate. The women, the children, the elders all participated. It is not about having an office. It is about going to the people. Sometimes communities asked us to come to help them solve problems they were facing. We would take our own food, but then people would kill a pig and feed us. That is how they started to accept us. We had discussions and that is how we started the *alcalde*s' association.

*Alcalde*s are the muscle of our people. The *alcalde*s in the 1980s [before the TAA was formed] were acting individually, and when they were acting individually, politicians could twist their leadership and could buy them. Thanks to the leaders who came next, *alcalde*s who followed the steps of our ancestors and got together and talked together in the *ab'ink*, things changed. That is the big achievement we have, being together and talking together. Conflicts and differences exist – that is normal; that happens in every family – but we fix that along the road.

Question: What is the role of customary governance and leadership?

Indigenous leadership is a kind of direct democracy. The way we make decisions is different from the state. The *ab'ink* [community assemblies] is where decisions are made. If it is a good decision, we share it. If it is a bad one, we share it too. In the end, the community takes ownership. If it is not working, we make another decision. We do not redo all decisions all the time, but if it is not working for us, we revisit it. We do not have to wait for anybody. It is a bottom-up approach. Indigenous leadership is driven by national party politics. It is up to the community

Figure 7 Maya village residents from young to old participate in an inter-community *ab'ink*, where communities come together to build unity and collectively discuss and democratically guide the struggle.

Credit: Roberto Kus, Maya Leaders Alliance

to decide, compared to the (state-based) village council, which is driven by two political parties. We do not wait for politicians to tell us anything.

You must have the capacity to become a good leader. We have a ladder you must climb (secretary, village police, second *alcalde*, first *alcalde*). You start as *alcalde*'s secretary and go through the levels. If people trust you, you will be made *alcalde*. Your leadership begins with your family. It is not because you are strong and outspoken. People look at your family life and how you conduct yourself. That is the difference, for example, with the (state-based) village councils.

As an Indigenous leader you are not the boss; you must serve. You must go the extra mile: you are not the chief, you are the servant. The *ab'ink* makes the decision. It is not the leader who is the chief, it is at the *ab'ink* where the decision is made (see Figure 7).

Question: What is the Maya struggle against – and what is it for?

Thematic answer: It is a struggle against erasure and dispossession.

It is about recognition and land security. It is a struggle against the perception of us as settlers. We are not seen as Belizeans. We do not sleep well when others tell us that. How can others say that to us? It is a struggle against being represented as squatters and against being treated as nobodies. We have value; we value what we have. We want to be recognised and respected. We have proof that our ancestors lived here. Maya sites show we are not settlers or squatters – we live here. The government needs to realise we are not settlers. We were already here before. We have lived here, enjoyed here. We are not fully recognised by the government. We must ask permission to visit Maya sites, but at the same time they are having 'Maya weddings' on these sites. It is a big profit for them. Tourists come to see Maya ruins, but when does the government respect our rights?

It is about defending ourselves from politicians and wealthy people who want to take away our resources. Some of the internal struggles are linked to politics and religion. These are things that divide us. Politicians are trying to divide us. Some religions divide us. We must realise that politicians are not here for us. These are some of the things we must focus on. Politicians want to demolish our rights. Right now, for example, a group of our own people organised a protest.[6] Those things do not really come from their heart. If the politicians do not tell them to do it or give them something, they do not do it. They just get bribed, but at the end of day, what do they achieve? Nothing.

Thematic answer: It is a struggle for land, community, and relations.

The Maya struggle starts with our land. It is about the security and well-being of Maya people, the land and culture of Maya people. It is about protecting life, land, and the future of our children. We do not want a situation where future generations will not have land. We want that for future generations. Land security.

We depend on the land – that is how we survive. Without land there is no food security. When we talk about Maya people and Maya life, we talk about forests, things we value – water, relations, connections . . . we have many practices. That is what we defend and safeguard. Without land there would be no Maya. Without land, we will not be able to provide for our families. We are nobody without land. To take away land from the Maya is to take away survival and life – it is to take away freedom.

Besides a struggle with the outside (e.g. government interference, third-party business interests, conservation that privatises communal lands), there is also an internal struggle. That struggle is about maintaining balance, which was there among us before. Unity was there before, respect for each other and respect for our [communal] land. That is the most vital one, the respect for our land and what comes from our land. That is a struggle with each other. It is a struggle

---

[6] Coinciding with the interview, a small group of Maya people connected to the state held a counterprotest against communal land rights.

about security in light of 'modern' life – land and food security, both individually and community-wise.

Thematic answer: It is a struggle for freedom and secure futures.

It is about the freedom that our ancestors had before colonialism. They had complete freedom; there was no threat. We are trying to get back and to give our children freedom. This includes freedom to elect our leaders (*alcaldes*).

For me, freedom would be where we have security on the land, food, rights … no prejudice. It is where my home is secure, and I can have that assurance. It includes mental, physical, social, and financial freedom – all that is needed for a civilisation, family-wise, community-wise, state-wise. It incorporates individual and community freedom. When all of that is there, I would say 'That is freedom.' If it is there, then I would say, 'Yes, it is worth it; we have less struggle now.' But if it is just only one component, then I would say the Maya struggle has not become real, because the freedom that I want is still not here. So, for me, freedom is the overall goal – from the state, internationally, and within us. When all of that is there, I can relax and say, 'The future is safe.' Freedom is for the future I want to see and know, because then I can say that my daughter and my daughter's daughters will be able to have these things.

Thematic answer: It is a struggle against co-optation and bribery.

All of us, presidents of the TAA, have all experienced attempts at bribing us. In 2013, during the election of the TAA president, someone who worked with the oil company went around offering *alcaldes* BZD 200 to vote for someone running against Mr Alfonso Cal, but Mr Alfonso won with an even bigger margin than before. Not long after each of us were elected, the Rural Development Ministry would call us, telling us to abandon our office and relationship with the MLA and the JCS. We would be offered air-conditioned offices and even vehicles.

When you are [an] *alcalde*, everyone comes when they see the richness of your land and they want to bribe you. If you do not stand for the Maya people, you will fall. They will come and say, 'Do that, do this. Follow us. We can help. . . .' It is really difficult. In my term, it was terrible. People would accuse me of taking money from the government and the oil company, but it was zero. Yes, they came, but I would not accept anything. And that is the hard part; not everybody can do it.

You see, the TAA does not allow itself to be dictated to by the ministry, because we have a position. Moreover, whatever the outcome of a meeting with the government or others is, we must go back to the assembly and inform community members. We must be directed by the assembly on how to move forward. That is how we work. The government says they will work together with us, but it never happens. They do not want to work with our leaders. I learnt this by going to Belmopan and the court . . . but the struggle continues.

One of the achievements we have among the *alcaldes* is that we are not easily corrupted. I think corruption is one of the sicknesses in organisations, and the *alcalde* system has the antivirus for that. If someone in the system gives in and is bought, the Maya system just cuts it and says take it; it is garbage already. I think this allows our system to continue and not be corrupted. It prevents selling out.

Question: Will the struggle continue, and what is on the horizon?

Our struggle is because of our people. If we do not have people, we do not have a struggle. Our struggle comes with three things: people, problems, and progress. You must see people. If you do not see people, I do not know what else you see. Our struggle is our people. We can make progress, but we must struggle. We can make progress, but we will have to go through many problems.[7] It is not easy. Our struggle needs leaders [who] believe in what we are aiming at. We have leaders [who] do not have a vision. They are just there. I tell our young people, understand our struggle. It is not easy. You cannot be tired and discouraged or join the other group. Like I say: people, problems, and progress.

Our struggle will continue because the state will always try to divide us; they will always go after our people. Money, and big people, big fishes will always find their way to our communities. Our struggle is not a short one; it is a long one. I may not see the end of our struggle, but I do not care if I die. I know it will happen. You will see it. It will happen. We will have joy at the end.

4 The Aspirations, Agency, and Resolve of Maya Women

This section is an abridged interview with Cristina Coc, a Q'eqchi' Maya activist, mother, and land defender from southern Belize who is also the spokesperson of the MLA. Throughout the discussion, Cristina underscores the pivotal roles played by Maya women in their communities, emphasising their agency, resilience, and integral contributions to cultural survival, place-making, spiritual practice, environmental stewardship, and social cohesion – despite facing systemic marginalisation. Highlighting deep connections to nature and the ways in which they are securing the well-being of

---

[7] *Alcalde*s are clear that progress related to the government respecting and recognising Maya land relations, customary governance, and their right to self-determination is slow and they face many challenges. They maintain their lands and freedom are constantly under attack, as is their unity, which is a priority that demands a great deal of time, energy, and resources.

future generations, Cristina illustrates how Maya women are pursuing gender justice and sustaining community and environmental relations.

Women's Roles in Defending Territory, Community, and Relations

Question: What role do Maya women play in community life and cultural survival? How do they preserve heritage and protect territory, and what do their relationships with the environment look like?

Maya women have long been the backbone of our communities and take on roles and responsibilities related to protecting, caregiving, and preserving relations for future generations. They are certainly more present in the community on a day-to-day basis and working in their homes, villages, and surroundings on a wide range of things related not only to taking care of the family, but Maya livelihoods, culture, and the environment in general. They maintain social ties and ultimately are trying to not only sustain and safeguard their families, but also their connections to and the overall well-being of the community (see Figure 8).

As a people, our culture and identity as *ral ch'och'* [being 'children of the Earth'] are defined by deep connections to the land which nurtures us and that we as a community nurture in return. Maya women understand this and do this daily, even though it is not always valued and is unpaid work. This dual role of

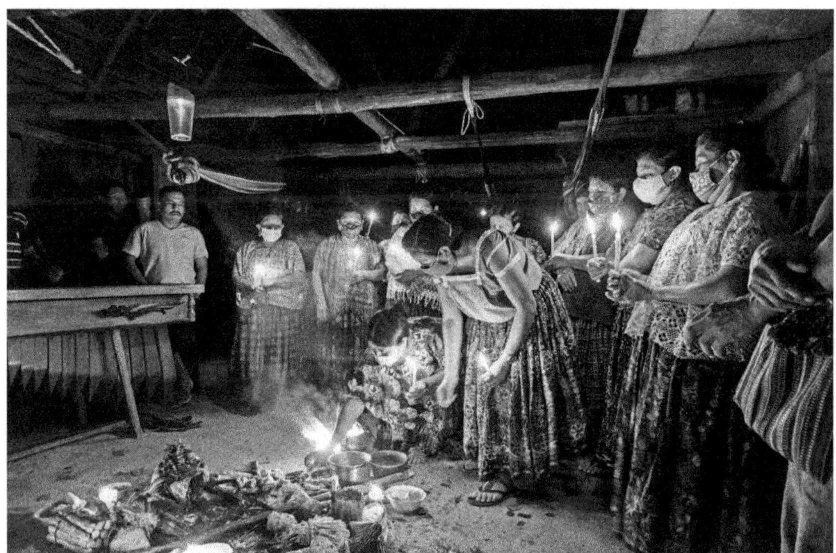

Figure 8 Maya women collectively lead and perform a fire ceremony at night in a rural village, which strengthens relations with the land, ancestors, memory, and the spiritual world.

Credit: Roberto Kus, Maya Leaders Alliance

caretaker and guardian is significant and sacred to us. It is passed down through generations and ensures the survival and continuation of our way of being. Our daily lives are connected to the rhythms of the natural and non-human world too, which is a relationship that informs our day-to-day practices, beliefs, and social systems.

Despite women's profound connection to the land and our pivotal role in community and environmental stewardship, capitalist notions of being 'modern' and 'developed' threaten to erode our customary ways of life, which are always changing and of course are not static. Land grabs, logging, deforestation, oil exploration, pollution, and even Western conservation initiatives are jeopardising the very forests and waters we depend upon. These things damage Maya heritage and disrupt our environmental relations. We are keepers of knowledge, from the medicinal properties of plants to traditional Maya agriculture and food production, as well as our ancestors' stories that are passed down from generation to generation. These all continue to guide our communities, and are our culture. This wisdom, while often overlooked by broader society, is crucial for the sustainability of our communities and the preservation and protection of the land, forests, water, and Maya heritage.

Water in particular is vitally important to women in a different way than it is to men and goes deeper than environmental protection because it is both spiritual and sustains life. I often hear women say: 'We are the ones that are the water protectors; we have to protect the water and we have to stop cutting trees around the water.' Typically, men tend to think of nature as a resource or thing to be controlled and might say: 'Oh, this is just a tree that is in my way,' and they would cut it down. Women will respond by saying: 'You know how long that [tree] has provided shade when I am washing my clothes? You know how long that has been the place where I hang my belongings when I come to the river? Do you know that the children grab and lean on that tree as they are climbing into the creek?' Women have a very intimate relationship with the environment and with keeping it clean, healthy, and alive, but water is especially important to women in a different way than it is to men.

Women also are the ones who predominantly harvest the copal resin, which is a sacred resin. Their relationship to that resin goes beyond what you can see physically and materially; it is spiritual – it is a respect for how things are. Women are also involved in traditional [Maya] agroecology. They are the ones who wake up early in the morning to select seeds – who protect the seeds – and ask and petition for a good harvest when there is planting taking place in the *milpa*. They are waking up early to do this, and yes, their husbands are there too, but the women are preparing everything. They are involved in the care of the upcoming harvest and next generation of seeds, and they are deeply concerned about these things.

You will see also that it is the women who do most of the work around the living quarters and compound. They are taking care of their homes and not only preparing but also growing food. From early morning trips to collect *jippa jappa* for both basket-weaving and to cook, selecting and saving seeds, processing *achiote*, washing clothes in the river, and helping with harvests, which bring us together in a spirit of cooperation and sharing, Maya women's actions are guided by an understanding of the land and the need to care for nature and the non-human world. Our gardens are often close to our homes too, which reveals our connection to the soil and provides sustenance as well as a space for talking, learning, and sharing traditional stories and knowledge.

On a daily basis, from early in the morning to late at night, women are doing the work that sustains relations, keeps the family healthy and nourished, and educates children. So the relationship they have with land is really tied to their futures. In their minds, when women think about the land and environment, they are not even thinking about just their own use – they are thinking about community health and their children. They ask themselves questions like: 'If we do not care for the land, what will I leave for my children, grandchildren, and their children? Will they be able to live good, happy lives? Will they be living in dignity?' I think these are unselfish acts and mindsets because they are thinking of and preserving future generations.

The bond we have with the land is also not transactional – it is sacred and encompasses respect for all living things and the cycles of life that sustain us. We teach our children to honour this relationship and instil in them values of stewardship and care for the forests, water, and environment. We see the land and all the gifts and richness it provides as a last hope for humanity, which must be respected and safeguarded. Overall, women are playing a pivotal role when it comes to defending community, territory, and Maya ways of being. This is evident in the many responsibilities we assume. Beyond nurturing children and managing the household, we are educators, healers, and spiritual guides. Our influence extends to the social relations of the village, where we act as mediators [and] peacekeepers and organise communal events. This community-building is vital, not only for cohesion but also for passing down customs, cultural values, and traditions (see Figure 9).

In many ways, women are the most generous to the community. You will see women who have jobs outside of the village – someone who is a teacher, for example – end up investing a great deal of income back into the community. They give freely and even do not feel discriminated against when they provide

Figure 9 Young Maya women in customary attire perform a traditional dance as a way to collectively sustain and celebrate community, cultural heritage, and the joys of life.

Credit: Roberto Kus, Maya Leaders Alliance

a fee for the *fahina*, which is communal work done for the collective benefit of the community.[8] They are not being asked or forced to contribute the fee, and even though they are not a man and might not have a husband to go to the *fahina*, they still want to help strengthen the village. They are also generous with their time in terms of when the community needs volunteers. Women may not be as vocal, but what you will see is that they show up and do everything they can to help. Their generosity and efforts go unrecognised, and I think this is one of the problems we must solve.

Confronting Patriarchy: Dreams of Dignity, Autonomy, and Respect

Question: What are pains and threats, and more importantly, dreams and aspirations of Maya women?

---

[8] The term *fahina* is derived from the Spanish word *faena*, which translates to 'task/work/chore'. For the Maya of southern Belize, it refers to formal occasions of communal work that maintain each community. On a regular basis, villages organise collective labour to ensure common areas are clean, safe, and flourishing. Men between certain ages are expected to contribute and fees are collected in certain circumstances. Participating in the *fahina* is a reminder that health, well-being, and survival are collective endeavours. Contributing to the *fahina*, physically and/or financially, is also evidence of one's connection and commitment to their community.

One thing I can say with certainty is that women across the world, regardless of background, face various internal and external challenges, pains, and threats due to patriarchy. Maya women do as well. Despite the critical role they play in the preservation of the environment and Maya culture, our voices are often marginalised in public spaces and governance, especially in matters related to policy and land management, whether it be nationally or at the village level. The decisions that shape the future of our communities and the resources we enjoy are frequently made without our input, overlooking our perspectives and the invaluable knowledge we bring to such discussions. The structure in place positions men above women, disregarding the fact that everyone is equal.

Women are also often perceived as inferior, a perception that extends into multiple spheres of life, including the home, workplace, and influential areas of decision-making. The ways in which women's intellect and contributions are devalued forces them to constantly have to prove their worth, not only to men but, regrettably, to other women as well. One of the most substantial obstacles Maya women encounter is the lack of recognition and value given to their input and participation, even when they are actively involved in the community. This exclusion does not deter us; instead, it strengthens our resolve. We find ways to share our knowledge and influence our communities, whether through informal networks or by teaching our children gender equality, as well as to have respect for the environment.

In my experience, our communities still struggle to fully embrace women's contributions to leadership and decision-making, as well as access to land. Despite the recognition some women achieve, they are often not the first choice for advice or ideas at home or the *ab'ink* (community assemblies). This preference leans towards men and such a patriarchal pattern is a point of pain and frustration that leads to numerous interconnected challenges for women, including being disempowered economically and not being able to access education. Even when women work, they rarely control all the finances and often must defer to men within the household. This dynamic is made worse when women lack a personal income themselves, which makes being financially dependent on men a barrier to pursuing their own dreams and aspirations.

In many communities, getting an education is particularly hard for girls. Often, even if a girl does exceptionally well in school, her family might still prioritise spending their limited resources on her brother's education. This is because of a deep-rooted belief that boys should be the ones to receive education, as they are expected to stay with their family and support them, while girls are seen as future members of another family once they marry. Witnessing this unfair treatment inspired me to start a scholarship programme that makes sure to support girls. This was also motivated by my own mother's story, who had dreamed of being a teacher but was arranged to be married, which cut her education short.

On a related matter, another aspect seldom discussed is the expectation for women to relocate to their husband's village or home, leading to isolation and dominance over women who find themselves without support in unfamiliar environments, sometimes even needing to navigate language barriers when moving from a Q'eqchi' to a Mopan Maya village or vice versa. My grandmother's experience reflects this. She married into a different community, which meant she had to adapt to a new language, mask her identity, wear different clothes, and adjust to new customs. These are some of the internal pains women experience, which often go unnoticed.

Healthcare is another challenge for Maya women, largely due to their lack of financial autonomy and decision-making power within their families. This often means their well-being is overlooked or ignored, with medical decisions, including those as basic as visiting a doctor, requiring approval from male family members. Bodily autonomy and the ability to make personal decisions is an obstacle for Maya women. They are constrained by rigid gender norms and their choices about life's major decisions – who to marry, whether to have kids, when to have children – are sometimes not solely theirs to make. Reproductive health and decisions about family size are particularly sensitive areas where women might feel unable to openly discuss their wishes with their husbands. Faced with these limitations, Maya women employ creative strategies to express their needs and assert their desires. They may need to rely on intermediaries, like a mother-in-law or godmother, to convey their health concerns or desires regarding children. Their resilience in overcoming these barriers is not just about fighting for their rights but also about ensuring a better, more equitable future for the next generation.

Maya villages also experience the same societal challenges that affect women all over, such as domestic violence, infidelity, and substance abuse – mainly alcohol for men – which are sensitive issues close to my heart yet difficult to address. Despite our united front in fighting for self-determination, land rights, and dignified lives, there is sometimes a reluctance to confront the issues of domestic violence and alcoholism amongst our communities. The challenges many Maya men face like discrimination, marginalisation, and the feelings they have about needing to assert their value and authority as men, often result in harm to those who are closest to them. They end up reacting, coping in destructive ways, and misdirecting their anger at others, often women. This is inexcusable and poses stressful challenges because the cycle of trauma is perpetuated but not talked about. The silence, because it is considered taboo, persists even among supportive men who are sympathetic about such matters. Avoidance becomes the easier path due to the discomfort and tensions that can emerge if the issues are confronted head-on.

The repercussions of the abuse extend to women *and* children, who bear the brunt of the violence and attempt to shield themselves from its impact. I believe it is crucial to instil in our sons from a young age the importance of recognising women's equality. This education should begin when they are infants, laying the foundation for them to grow into men who see no issue in performing acts of service, whether it is making breakfast for their children or even preparing a woman a cup of coffee in public, regardless of onlookers. Such behaviour may seem minor, but it challenges and changes deeply ingrained social norms that favour men. It suggests that our traditional gender roles need [to be] re-evaluated. It is about more than just personal actions and individual behaviours too. Engaging communities in altering behaviours and attitudes is essential, and this change can be reinforced not only at home but also at schools and community gatherings. Teachers and village leaders play a fundamental role in this. Those of us in positions of authority and influence must actively work to ensure that women are not marginalised and given the same opportunities as men.

In many ways, the heart of the struggle for Maya women is the battle for their own self-determination and autonomy – to have their voices, ideas, and desires be heard, respected, and taken seriously. In our homes, where safety and peace should be a given, we often encounter our first hard lessons of inequality. Women's voices are diminished, sometimes criticised, and our contributions undervalued. This sidelining is not confined to the domestic space and home either; it extends into the village assemblies, community spaces, and across Belizean society, where despite possessing the same capabilities, women's leadership and opinions take a back seat to those of men. Despite the challenges and pains I just mentioned, things are slowly beginning to shift. Through education initiatives and collective organising, Maya women are gradually changing things. It is important for men to be active supporters and a part of the process. Women are not only advocating for their individual rights but also demonstrating the importance of the entire community listening to and respecting women's choices and ideas.

As far as the aspirations of Maya women, they mirror those we have for communities and ourselves: safety, peace, and the ability and opportunity to thrive. We envision communities where harmony prevails and where women are not taken for granted and can pursue their dreams without fear or stigma. This dream extends beyond the pursuit of individual success; it encompasses a desire for communal well-being and community flourishing. Maya women across the villages are very resourceful, generous, and hospitable. We can

Figure 10 Village members make space and listen attentively to women's voices in the struggle at a Maya Day event whilst celebrating *aj' ral ch'och' (being 'children of the Earth).*

Credit: Roberto Kus, Maya Leaders Alliance

manage unexpected situations and frequently welcome guests and prepare meals rapidly, seemingly out of nothing. This shows how creative and caring we can be. If given the chance, we could use these skills to help our whole community in governance.

In many ways, I think many Maya women would like to see their kindness, generosity, and sacrifices reciprocated and offered back to them. We dream of communities where women's voices, ideas, hard work, contributions, and leadership are valued, welcomed, and respected – both in the domestic space of the home and the broader arenas of governance and decision-making (see Figure 10). It's a tough journey marked by both small victories and ongoing struggles, but the strength and determination of Maya women are paving the way for meaningful change.

5 Maya Youth: Exploring *Se' Komonil* and *Sahil Ch'oolej*

Amplifying Maya Youth Voices through 'Desire-Based Research'

In the spirit of respecting and valuing diverse forms of Indigenous knowledge and integrated (non-Western) approaches to well-being, this section at once foregrounds the voices of Maya youth and their concerns about the future. To do so, we share findings from 'desire-based research' (Tuck, 2009) that has been co-designed by Maya organisers from the MLA and local village members across Toledo District. Specifically, our iterative participatory process, which has now spanned more than five years and involves a recurring series of annual projects, employs creative arts-based methods as a means of documenting the 'joys, pains, and dreams' of Maya youth. A key focus has also been placed on exploring young people's thoughts regarding environmental relations, *se' komonil, aj ral ch'och'*, and *sahil ch'oolej*, a Q'eqchi' term that roughly translates to 'peace-joy-flourishing' (Miss et al., 2021). Markedly, the idea and driving force behind exploring and documenting the 'joys, pains, and dreams' is a particular area of research that has been developed by organisers in the MLA alongside non-Indigenous partners.

Methodologically, the longitudinal process has included arts-based dreaming exercises developed by Maya collaborators, walking go-along interviews, inter-active games, participatory film, and public youth presentations (Gahman, Penados, Greenidge, et al., 2020). Over the past few years, the ongoing initiative has also featured a series of photovoice projects, which is our focus here. Notably, non-Indigenous collaborators continue to contribute to the research after receiving training on cultural safety protocols, which serves as a safeguard against 'parasitic research' (Odeny and Bosurgi, 2022) and pathologising 'damage-centered' approaches (Tuck, 2009). On a broader political level, then, the data generated and the empirical findings presented in what follows are the direct product of Indigenous epistemological processes and the political agency of the Maya people of southern Belize, which highlight the primacy they, especially youth, place on their connections to local forests, waters, ecosystems, and interdependent human–environment relations (Smith, Penados, and Gahman, 2022).

With respect to investigating the agency and perspectives of youth on the notions of *se' komonil, aj ral ch'och'*, and *sahil ch'oolej*, we have worked with more than fifty Maya young people to date to discuss issues affecting their communities and aspirations. In conjunction with local Maya organisers, we tailored the research to include the following generative prompts:

- What are the joys, pains, dreams, and desired futures of Maya youth?
- What significance do culture, heritage, and land carry for youth?
- How can youth further develop organising and leadership capacities?

In addition to these key queries, sustainability, community health, concerns about climate change, and emotions young people experience regarding forests and local waters all featured heavily. One of the prevailing themes that emerged across this photovoice project was the relational importance of nature, well-being, and connections Maya youth as Indigenous people maintain with the environment, their ancestors, and culture. A partial selection of the images and narratives provided by the youth participants about 'health and well-being', 'living a good life', and 'environmental relations' is offered next.

Reciprocity, Gift-Stewardship, and Integrated Approaches to Health

For the Maya youth who participated in the research, *health* is an expansive term and maintaining optimal well-being of the land provides the resources necessary to maintain human life. In their eyes, the relationship between humans and nature is one of reciprocity and interdependency wherein a deterioration of one leads to a deterioration of the other. Centring mutuality as a foundation upon which to build relationships with land means that seemingly discrete entities and distinct phenomena (e.g. land, people, forests, community, gender relations) actually appreciably impact each other. In other words, for the participants, ecological health is needed for human health, which is reflected by Ximena, who discusses the interconnections between gender and human–environment interdependence.

> I took this photo because it seems very important to us, the women, and everybody in each community to bathe. And it is most commonly us, the women and young girls, who do laundry. It applies to the communities to get drinks and to go fishing for our own foods. We can improve by keeping it healthier and by protecting it from pollution so that we keep the river clean. (see Figure 11)

Figure 11 Ximen's photo

Relationship with the land was spoken about by participants frequently and in reciprocal terms, particularly in discussions about deforestation, pollution, and contamination. For example, many of the youth expressed a sentiment that if you look after the land, the land will look after you, which is conveyed by Julian's narrative.

> If people followed what was on this sign, it would help them live a better life in the future. There would be less garbage and less garbage flies, and people would be healthier. (see Figure 12)

All the youth described rivers and waterways as culturally significant and life-giving. Water is viewed as a source of social reproduction and psycho-spiritual well-being through its community-sustaining properties, which include washing, bathing, fishing, relaxation, reflection, and recreation. This links with both Ximena's previously cited comment and Isidora's to come, who both stated that the river needs to be kept healthy in order to sustain a variety of human activities, not to mention the overarching sense of serenity, peace, and tranquillity that water provides.

> This waterfall is full of joy. Water is full of good things which Maya people can survive with. They can fish and that can feed them. Women go to the river to wash dishes, wash their clothes, and bathe. They can also drink it. People have populated riverbanks for centuries since water is vital to life. The fresh, clean river has been the essential source of water for generations of Maya. The river provides fish and snails for eating and is a place for washing clothes and dishes, bathing, and recreation. (see Figure 13)

Figure 12 Julian's photo

Figure 13 Isadora's photo

Despite the water systems that have been installed in the villages, women still go to the river to do laundry. Wash is done on a large flat rock in the river which serves as tables. Clothes are hand-washed and rinsed in the river water. This task takes the average woman one to two hours every day. Families also go to the river to bathe. It is common to see children running in the morning to wash before school and men hurrying to the river to beat the sunset when they get back from their farms.

Thinking of land as an inalienable and reciprocal good at the heart of a 'gift economy', Maya youth participants often thought of their own human–environment relationships as something akin to stewardship. To describe the land as a sacred and ancestral gift meaningfully alters how land is perceived. Doing so moves away from worldviews and conceptual frameworks that reify land as a commodity and private property to be individually possessed, owned, bought, and sold. Conversely, perceiving land and 'Mother Earth' (a not uncommon term across Maya communities) as inherited territory, a living gift, and shared commons that is the basis of and nurtures collective well-being, sustains not only social relations but also Maya expressions of spirituality, kinship, and culture. For example, both Luciana and Alejandro describe land and heritage sites (e.g. Maya temples) as intergenerational gifts passed on for caretaking and crucial for the living memory, history, heritage, and ancestral bonds of the Maya people.

Figure 14 Luciana's photo

Lubaantun is a place that is very good to go and visit. The reason why I chose this site is because there you can go and see the different things and structures that our ancestors have left for us as a young generation. (see Figure 14)

This picture reminds me about our ancestors and what they have left to us. The picture is an altar for the Mayas who were living before and some are still living now too. They used this altar to pray to their god. ... As a student I want to know the history of the Maya ancestors, so we should have more visits. It is my culture and I also ask the old people to learn more about our history. (see Figure 15)

Both Luciana and Alejandro connect the passing of land stewardship, ancestral memory, and the significance of sacred sites with the desire to learn more of their heritage, which signals that the land is a source of cultural, spiritual, and environmental knowledge for Maya youth. Thinking in terms of stewardship reflects a particular ontology wherein the natural environment and non-human world are perceived as living entities offering gifts dend abundance to people and communities if treated with respect and gratitude (i.e. if customary Maya responsibilities and duties to the land are observed).

The youth also showed aspirations towards maintaining strong Maya-based institutions including systems of education, environmental management, and

Figure 15 Alejandro's photo

healthcare. For example, Vicente, in speaking of the significance of land and its inextricable links to livelihood for the Maya, states:

> So what I feel about this picture is joy and happiness because we, the Maya people, still have our forest and take care of it. In other parts of the world, Indigenous people do not own land, which is hard. So to the Maya it is like a supermarket to use because everything we need comes from the forest: food and resources. The challenges in the Maya community are some people doing illegal logging and forest fires. (see Figure 16)

Although not necessarily explicitly stated as such, Vicente observes and contemplates major political-economic issues in his narrative while offering solidarity to other disproportionately affected Indigenous groups who are experiencing dispossession, land grabs, and extractivist violence. He explores two things: firstly, he references the forest as a (non-commoditised) 'supermarket', and secondly, he points to Maya land management practices, traditional food systems, agroforestry, and regenerative cultivation practised by Maya farmers in their *milpas* as sustainable care, which is evidenced by research (Downey et al., 2023). Land is understood as a gift provided by the Creator; there is access to food, medicine, water, and shelter within the vast layers of the 'supermarket' (forest) Vicente speaks of. All the youth emphasised that the forest had been passed down to them by their ancestors and was meant to be enjoyed, used, taken care of, replenished, and treated with reverence as a key

Figure 16 Vicente's photo

aspect of their (bio-)cultural heritage – not extracted from, depleted, and treated as a taken-for-granted object or merchandise.

A sense of health and wellness can also be achieved by remembering traditional practices of medicine, in addition to acknowledging the benefits of biomedical approaches. Upon reflecting on a photograph she took of her local community and rural village life, Valentina expresses the need for healthcare infrastructure that does not mean losing one's cultural identity.

> We need a clinic for our health and also for other people who need it. Long ago, the Maya did not take pills as we do nowadays. Before, they used to look for leaves to mash and drink. They were bush doctors before. But also, the satellite clinic can also help in many ways. It is getting better and I want it to get much better in the future, but I am afraid of losing our identity. (see Figure 17)

Implied in Valentina's narrative is a search for various forms of knowledge that are able to sit side by side, striking a balance between biomedical systems and traditional and ancestral methods of healing. Similarly, this sentiment is extended to traditional forms of land management and agroforestry, which was expressed by both Ramona and Maria, who describe the sustainable practice of swidden (slash-and-char) agriculture in *milpa*s of the Maya people and just how important learning the technique and science behind agroecology from seasoned farmers and local elders is for youth.

Figure 17 Valentina's photo

The younger generation should bring back the slash-and-burn (i.e. slash-and-char). It is a part of my community, but sometimes the person who is burning is not there and the fire spreads to other people's farms. It should be done by a person who knows how to do it and that has time to do it so they can teach us (Maya youth), and we could learn to do it ourselves. Our parents, grandparents, and the older generation know how to do it and take care of the land. (see Figure 18)

The cacao tree is an important element to Maya life. It reminds me of our ancestors because that is what they used to drink. All of the people living in this community are Maya. In today's society, it is only the elders that are planting cacao. More trees could be planted by gathering all Maya youths and seeking assistance for the seeds. Some families make chocolate from it and sell it too. The cacao drink is healthy and also a channel for youth to reconnect with our ancestors to maintain our traditions. Us youths may well accomplish this by gathering with our elders to continue traditional knowledge. (see Figure 19)

Ramona and Maria's narratives demonstrate a desire for integrated approaches to planetary health and sustainable land management that are rooted in the intergenerational transmission of place-based ecological knowledges and the preservation of the Maya's dynamic cultural heritage. On this point, throughout our conversations and their group reflections, Maya youth consistently expressed a desire to sustain and (re)vitalise Maya livelihood strategies, territorial connections, ancestral memories, and methods of offering stewardship to

Figure 18 Ramona's photo

Figure 19 Maria's photo

the land. In short, as was expressed in the closing spiritual ceremonies of several of our photovoice projects, the youth felt their identity as Indigenous Maya people – and in particular as *aj ral ch'och'* – was equally a source of pride and something worth fighting for and protecting.

Figure 20 Roselia's photo

Across the board, and despite the challenges their communities are facing with respect to colonial legacies, racist discrimination, and the ever-present threat of land grabs detailed in the preceding sections, the Maya youth maintained a still and steadfast sense of optimism, joy, and hope about their place in the world and future to come, as is evidenced in Roselia's reflection.

> These flowers bring me joy. When I see them, I remember how my parents and family and others treat me. Our community and the forest are beautiful. It all makes me feel glad about my future in the world as a young girl. It looks bright – like how I am trying my best to further my education and become someone. This photo symbolises the love I have for my parents, family, friends, nature, and others. (see Figure 20)

A Reflection on the Joys, Pains, and Dreams of Maya Young People

In sum, through participatory creative methods, an Indigenous epistemological approach, and collective ways of producing knowledge found amongst Maya villages, the activities detailed throughout this section aspired to magnify youth voices and motivate young people to become more involved in co-creating the realities within which they will live their lives and ultimately pass on to subsequent generations. On this point, we think it only fitting to end this section with a joint narrative co-authored by Maya youth from Toledo District who have worked alongside us for several years. In relationally reflecting upon the 'joys, pains, and dreams' of Indigenous young people in general, as well as their own local context, they write:

> On a global scale, governments need to concretely address the pressing threat of climate change. State officials must listen to Indigenous people. Indigenous people are keepers and guardians of the land. On an intrinsic level, we understand that Mother Earth is not a resource to be owned. This is a deep contrast to the conventional approaches to 'development' that are driven by capitalism. We know how to care for Mother Earth just as She cares for us. The land is life. The land is our future. The land breathes life.
>
> Locally, here in Toledo District, the Maya are mobilizing and strengthening communities to construct a future of *se' komonil* and *sahil ch'oolej*. We are overcoming challenges, working through pain, and remembering our ancestors all at once in order to build a future that is created by Maya people – for Maya people. It is embedded in the heart of the Maya people to do everything we can to secure the well-being of our villages and future generations. It is our right and obligation, especially the youth, to continue this fight to challenge what the government and corporations are doing to the environment, our lands, and our communities, as well as the earth. As we have said, our struggle is not just for land rights, but against the destruction of the planet and for a better world. In the midst of this, *se' komonil* and *sahil ch'oolej* have kept our lights ever burning as we continue to cast our dreams of a sustainable and just Maya future.
>
> Joy for Maya youth, in the context of our local communities and the grand challenges we face, is something that can be viewed from two different angles. Firstly, within our villages, the things that bring us joy is our Maya identity, families, farms, land, traditions, and *se' komonil*. We must hold on to our notion of joy as Maya people and never diminish it as a value worth pursuing. Our communities are strong and focused on building a partnership with the government to better our communities, and in the grand scheme of things, the entire country. Presently, though, this is our pain: the government is the biggest barrier we face in our political fight for basic human and land rights. Secondly, amongst our communities, the thing that cannot be taken away from us is our resilience, which is a product of *se' komonil*, mobilising, and our dreams. We, like Indigenous peoples over the world, endure harsh realities. This is especially true of our youth, who are a target for eradication in the capitalist world. For Indigenous communities, youth are the key to the continuation of our traditions, values, and knowledges. We must continue to resurface and challenge capitalism because it is suffocating the world.
>
> In conclusion, our parents and ancestors have taught us that with *se' komonil* we can make it through the adversity we face and find *sahil ch'oolej*. We must not stray from our values. Despite the challenges we face, we have joy. We must always remember that family, land, and community bring greater joy. We dream of our people always having *sahil ch'oolej* and *se' komonil*. Importantly, amidst everything we experience, be it pain or joy, there is a need for youth to remain

positive, resolute, and realise that their dreams can indeed come to fruition – and that the dream of seeing their communities change positively is a joy that can neither be bought nor sold. This also gives us deeper insight into the future to come; we are going to create a future that is rooted in what will bring the world more peace, well-being, and *sahil ch'oolej*.

6 Combatting Colonial Legacies and Climate Injustice

This section is an edited interview with Pablo Mis, a Q'eqchi' Maya organiser from southern Belize with the MLA and the current programme director of the JCS. In discussing the historical and contemporary challenges faced by the Maya people, Pablo situates their realities against a backdrop of colonial legacies and global Indigenous struggles for land and self-determination. He also references the groundbreaking 2015 CCJ judgment that affirmed customary Maya land rights, emphasising that it was not only a significant victory for Indigenous people in Belize, but also a precedent-setting case for the entire Caribbean and step in the right direction with respect to climate justice. Regarding vulnerability environmental relations and the climate crisis, Pablo speaks about the Maya people's role as guardians of the forest and contributions to stewardship, sustainability, and conservation (see Figure 21).

Figure 21 A *milpa* amidst the mountains and tropical forest of southern Belize. Maya agroecological science and organic intercropping has sustained livelihoods and culture for generations.

Credit: Roberto Kus, Maya Leaders Alliance

The Historical and Contemporary Challenges
of the Maya People

Question: Can you give us an overview of your work and the historical to present-day challenges the Maya face with respect to defending their ancestral territories, communities, and relations?

Greetings from the lands of the Maya people in southern Belize. It is my pleasure to be speaking on the important question you have raised. First off, I want to express my solidarity to all Indigenous brothers and sisters, to the many local communities out there who have stood defiant in ensuring that we do our duty and fulfil our responsibility as Indigenous people to actively participate in creating a world where many worlds fit. This is something that we owe to the children of our children, and we must ensure we are constantly reaching out and connecting with others.

The Q'eqchi' and Mopan Maya of southern Belize have collectively struggled to demand recognition as First Peoples of the land that is now Belize. This recognition, of course, is based on ... aspiration and ability: we must take charge of our lives to contribute deliberately to the forming of communities and societies where we feel that each and every person is cared for, has a chance at making a living, and is able to live a dignified, good life. Now, what I have just said is often easy to speak of in words, but actually very difficult to live and experience. This has come in the face of organised attempts by various entities – for example, the government, third-party actors, [and] multinational corporations that have interest in the resources of Maya lands.

Despite all we have been through, we are fortunate to have a strong system of customary governance, the *alcaldes*, one that goes back to pre-contact, precolonial days and makes decisions through community assemblies known as *ab'inks*. It is a system that allows us to be community – and to be accountable to community. It is also an Indigenous Maya institution that I think the government wishes did not exist because it sees it as a threat and obstacle. For the Maya people, though, it is a consistent, stable, and democratic system that allows us to join our thoughts and voices for taking a stand for what we think is right in terms of correcting historical wrongs and pursuing land rights and self-determination.

On a day-to-day basis, our work is widespread and community-based, but perhaps the singular most important priority we have is to be able to live free – to live without fear on our land. Years back, there was a time when our leaders realised the discrimination and marginalisation we experience as Indigenous people place us at a disadvantage given the fact that we find ourselves within recently drawn colonial borders. Our leaders quickly understood that, as much as we dream of being a part of the mainstream economy, public education, and healthcare system, we realised that – in the absence of being free in our lands – we will not be living the lives we desire.

So, for the last thirty years, our efforts have shifted to ensuring that we protect our existence on our ancestral lands. We are focused on building and strengthening our ever-evolving Maya institutions and the strength of our communities on this land. We also are using strategic litigation and international legal standards that have been established to advance, and in many ways, force the government to comply with obligations it has accepted as a part of the global community to recognise and respect Indigenous land rights. I offer all of this just to set out the stage that our work within the Maya communities is varied but related to all these things. It is work that we believe is singularly important if we are to continue existing as Maya Q'eqchi' and Mopan people.

Since 2015 specifically, we have been locked into negotiations regarding the implementation of the CCJ court order. We believe it is important for the entire Caribbean to pay attention to the case of the Maya people because it sets the parameters regarding jurisprudence for Indigenous people's rights within the region. That said, it is not solely about Maya land rights because our case is built upon internationally accepted norms and standards. Many countries, including many across the Caribbean, have signed onto international human rights accords and declarations. Part of what we are seeing, then, is that the Maya people have learned to utilise legal mechanisms, treaties, and judicial processes in contemporary times to hold the government to account.

In many respects, we, as Indigenous people and citizens, like other Indigenous people, are shaping and advancing the human rights obligations of the countries we now find ourselves in. We feel this is a positive thing in terms of protecting constitutional rights not only for the Maya, but [also for] all Belizeans and other groups across the region. Our particular land rights case has been marred by bad faith on the part of the government and partisan politics. For years, closed-door concessions to third parties, encroachments onto communal lands, and FPIC violations have all continued. It is important to emphasise to other Indigenous people that it is going to be almost impossible to realise and build Indigenous communities through imposed colonial institutions and foreign governance mechanisms. The very existence of such political structures and systems (e.g. Westminster-modelled states) [is] inherently contrary and opposed to Indigenous systems of governance.

Racial Discrimination, Representation, and the Climate Crisis

Question: What major crises and forms of injustice are the Maya people experiencing, and how are the communities collectively intervening and confronting them both regionally and locally?

Indigenous communities in the Caribbean and Latin America, like their counterparts worldwide, are currently navigating a wide range of challenges. These span from land grabs, environmental degradation, and the loss of cultures and languages, to ongoing battles against racial discrimination and denials of customary governance systems. My reflections on these issues are shaped by personal experiences and the broader collective actions of Indigenous peoples worldwide. There are systemic barriers and rigid mindsets that exacerbate the stigma, adversity, and obstacles we all face. While the roots of these challenges are historical wrongs dating back to colonial contact, they are compounded by government policies that often disregard the unique situations and grassroots voices of Indigenous people.

One long-standing issue is related to representation – or rather, a lack thereof – of Caribbean Indigenous peoples in international forums, particularly those concerning discussions of preserving forests, loss and damage, and climate action. The under-representation is not due to apathy or an absence of effort or interest on the part of Indigenous communities. Rather, it is a product of structural forces that limit our participation. For instance, in recent global climate negotiations, the mutual stance of Caribbean states seldom reflects the nuanced perspectives and specific needs of Indigenous peoples from the region. The position of Indigenous people globally, just like the Maya people here in Belize, is that we have a role to play in defending the environment and shaping climate policy because we are the ones who are from and among the forests.

An Indigenous brother of mine from Guyana once joked in frustration, 'Well, you know the issue is that governments did not form in the forest.' What he meant by this is that Indigenous people's participation in climate negotiations remains on the margin, even though we are from the land, yet state officials continue to be in the driver's seat but rarely spend time in the forest. This highlights a significant gap between lived realities, local knowledges, and policy influence, as well as highlights the urgent need for more government awareness and accountability. We also need stronger alliances and collaborative efforts among Indigenous groups, both within the Caribbean and at the global scale.

Efforts to establish an alliance of Indigenous people across the region stress the importance of solidarity in our struggles. Such an alliance would amplify our collective voice and enable us to share experiences, strategies, and ideas more effectively. On this point, recent legal successes in Guyana, Belize, and Honduras offer us all hope and demonstrate the power of united action. Beyond environmental advocacy and political engagement, the fight against racial discrimination remains a critical front for Indigenous communities. The use of derogatory language, negative stereotypes, and other prejudices by public officials not only disrespects Indigenous cultures, but also perpetuates a legacy of oppressive racism that dates back to colonialism. We are portrayed as irrational threats to national cohesion and being opposed to 'development'.

For example, here the Maya have been accused on several occasions of 'Balkanising Belize', which makes no sense whatsoever considering what the term actually means. And regionally, the increasing number of murdered Indigenous activists clearly reveals the dangers faced by Indigenous communities who are advocating for land rights and defending ancestral territories. The persistence of this violence underscores the need for continued vigilance and collective action against institutionalised racism. Despite international condemnation, the discrimination persists, and government officials often refuse to engage in respectful dialogue. Addressing issues like this requires a concerted effort from Indigenous groups, their allies, and the international community.

In confronting these challenges, the wisdom of our elders and resilience of our communities are indispensable. Our collective endeavours are aimed not only at survival, but [also] at forging a future where Indigenous peoples can thrive, preserve our cultural heritage, and safeguard forests and waterways for generations to come. What we are facing now is a critical juncture that calls for unity, for elevating our voices, and for collective action. We must demand the respect, recognition, and rights that have been denied to Indigenous peoples for far too long.

Back to the specific issue of the climate crisis: there is scientific research and evidence that has shown that lands occupied and managed by Indigenous people are some of the most biodiverse places in the world. It is also important to note that where Indigenous land rights are recognised and protected – there are healthy lands and communities. By healthy lands and communities, I mean that communities are meeting their basic needs and caring for each other, as well as caring for watersheds, rivers, forests, and *milpa*s (see Figure 22). There is evidence this is the global reality and it's actually the same story for southern Belize.

If you fly over Belize, for instance, you will see that much of the remaining forests are where Maya communities reside. This is something that is very important to us and, in fact, we have a saying here: 'healthy lands, healthy forests; healthy people, healthy communities'. That's often something we always speak of. My daughter now always talks about the concept of *ral ch'och'*. We continue to say we are *ral ch'och'*, literally 'the children of Mother Earth'. So this is not merely a matter of having access to land as an object or private property; we are aspiring to protect our very provider, our Mother, because without it we cannot survive.

Figure 22 A veteran Maya farmer with expertise in regenerative agroforestry carries seed and uses a planting stick to sow corn in anticipation of the ever-shifting seasonal rains.

Credit: Roberto Kus, Maya Leaders Alliance

Indigenous Knowledges and Relations as Effective Climate Action

Question: In focusing on the realities of the climate crisis, what should readers know about how it is impacting Indigenous people globally, as well as the Maya communities specifically in Belize?

Firstly, it is well established that climate change is not impacting everyone equally. While the crisis is global, the most devastating effects are disproportionately falling on Indigenous communities – those who for millennia have lived in careful balance with their surrounding ecosystems. The environmental relations and values of many Indigenous cultures – from their reliance on forests, rivers, and local seeds for subsistence to the cultural and spiritual significance of landscapes – make them extremely vulnerable to the disruptions caused by climate change. Indigenous communities around the world have developed ecological knowledge systems that allow them to adapt to changing environments and various disasters.

This is not simply abstract knowledge but a complex lived understanding of ecosystems, seasonal patterns, and the interconnectedness of species. Sadly, this deep understanding, which offers invaluable lessons for climate change mitigation and adaptation strategies, is often overlooked or undervalued by policymakers and even conservationists. Consider the situation in Belize, a small nation with a long history of tension between Indigenous land rights and government-led development agendas. The Maya people secured an unprecedented legal victory in the CCJ that affirmed their ancestral rights. However, years later, the government continues to demonstrate a concerning lack of urgency in implementing the decision.

The lack of respect for Indigenous land tenure not only jeopardises the heritage and cultural survival of the Maya, but also has widespread environmental consequences. Securing and protecting Indigenous land rights is intrinsically linked to sustainable land management practices and conservation. When Indigenous people can manage their territories freely and according to their traditional practices, which they also continue to expand and innovate upon, they act as guardians against deforestation, biodiversity loss, and the exploitation of Mother Earth.

The pressing need to centre Indigenous perspectives in the fight against climate change extends far beyond Belize. Across the globe, a shift in power dynamics is necessary. Meaningful inclusion means upholding commitments like the United Nations Declaration on the Rights of Indigenous Peoples (UNDRIP) and FPIC protocol as bare minimums. Financial support for conservation projects led by Indigenous communities, legal protection for ancestral lands, a seat at the table, and being taken seriously in high-level climate negotiations are all essential.

The invaluable contribution of many Indigenous worldviews stems from a holistic way of understanding the planet, where humanity and nature are inseparable and not severed from each other. The land management techniques, regenerative forms of agroforestry, and stories and teachings passed down from Indigenous elders to youth all promote respect for the Earth. By supporting intergenerational learning and local science within Indigenous communities, we are safeguarding a wealth of knowledge that is more relevant than ever, especially given the intensifying climate crisis.

All that said, mere recognition of the importance of Indigenous approaches is insufficient.[9] Centuries of colonialism, forced displacement, and the criminalisation and denigration of Indigenous governance systems and cultural practices have left a legacy of harm and mistrust. To pave the way for respectful collaboration, we need to depart from institutions that marginalise and ridicule Indigenous voices. Land titling, the return of sacred sites, and a tangible commitment to correcting historical wrongs are critical steps to create conditions where Indigenous-led climate solutions and sustainability practices can flourish.

There is also a need to critically examine Western conservation models that, despite being well intentioned, are sometimes counterproductive. Historically,

---

[9] Scholars like Coulthard (2014) caution against a mere politics of recognition for achieving self-determination, and in a similar vein, Indigenous movements like that of the Zapatistas avow that ultimately the target is overcoming colonial modernity/capitalist annihilation (Gahman, 2020).

efforts to create 'untouched' wilderness and wild land areas have displaced the very Indigenous communities who have been the most effective stewards of those environments. Fair and effective conservation practices must move away from the idea of separating humans from nature and instead acknowledge Indigenous communities as stewards and protectors of forests and ecosystems. I must also say that Indigenous people are not simply victims of climate change. We are essential knowledge holders, resourceful innovators, and the frontline defenders of the world's most biodiverse forests and habitats. Our and the planet's survival are inextricably linked.

Overall, in my parting words, I want to emphasise that Indigenous people have historically possessed distinct and sophisticated systems of governance, economies, and connections to the environment. These relations and worldviews are rooted in centuries of evolving traditions and intergenerational knowledges, which hold invaluable insight for addressing current global challenges – especially climate change. Since colonial contact up to the present day, we have always been preached at about how those in power have 'modern' ideas about 'developing' and 'advancing' society, yet they continue to only make things worse.

It is crucial, now more than ever, that we recognise and learn from Indigenous knowledges and relationships with the environment (see Figure 23). By doing so,

Figure 23 A river used and enjoyed by the Maya for fishing, washing, and leisure. Community residents care for, communally share, and steward such spaces to ensure sparkling waters and flourishing forests.

Credit: Roberto Kus, Maya Leaders Alliance

we not only respect the rights and dignity of Indigenous communities, but [we] will also find better solutions for the health of our planet and all of humanity. In today's world, it is urgent that Indigenous people reclaim our power and rightful place, as well as assert our role in shaping the future. Building solidarity and fostering unity are fundamental. Seeing our Indigenous brothers and sisters putting their lives on the line and bravely standing up for their rights is inspiring and highlights our collective responsibility to contribute to a better world.

7 The Uses, Limitations, and Colonial Paradox of FPIC

The FPIC Protocol, International Law, and Indigenous Rights

The FPIC concept and protocol have emerged globally as a mechanism that promises to protect the well-being of Indigenous lands and people. It is also framed as an instrument through which Indigenous communities can exercise certain aspects of self-determination. As a principle enshrined in international law, FPIC primarily aims to safeguard and empower Indigenous communities by ensuring they are informed and agree to any activities that will affect their territories, cultures, and livelihoods prior to the commencement of any given development project (Tomlinson, 2019).

In Belize, the landmark decision by the CCJ in 2015 affirming Maya land rights also ordered the application of an FPIC protocol. This thrust FPIC into the national and regional spotlight, where it quickly became and remains a controversial lightning rod and contested terrain. At present, violations and the weaponisation of FPIC by the Belizean government reveal the degree to which good faith consultation and culturally appropriate consent procedures are consistently elided and contravened. Accordingly, given how significant and contentious FPIC has become in relation to the Maya struggle, this section critically examines the protocol's uses, contradictory limitations, and coloniality.

The right to FPIC is a fundamental principle in international law designed to shield Indigenous communities and cultures from potential adverse impacts related to activities that take place on their traditional lands (Leifsen et al., 2017). It was first recognised under the International Labour Organisation's (ILO) Convention 169 in 1989, which marked a pioneering step in legally acknowledging Indigenous rights concerning development. Later, FPIC was appreciably expanded by UNDRIP in 2007, which emphasised the necessity of obtaining consent for any economic projects, legislative actions, or national security measures that would affect Indigenous groups (Ward, 2011), and also stressed to governments worldwide the importance of respecting Indigenous people's ancestral lands, sovereignty, and customary decision-making processes.

Relatedly, in 2016, the American Declaration on the Rights of Indigenous Peoples (ADRIP) further reinforced FPIC by underscoring its relevance in the Americas by aiming to guarantee the protection of Indigenous territories and cultures. Jointly, these international instruments affirm FPIC as a critical mechanism to ensure that Indigenous communities have a decisive voice in projects and activities that will affect their livelihood strategies, local ecosystems, and cultural heritage (Wright and Tomaselli, 2019). Notably, at the core of FPIC lies the principle of self-determination (Yaffe, 2018), which has been incorporated into several key international agreements including the International Covenant on Economic and Social Rights, the International Covenants on Civil and Political Rights, and the broader United Nations Charter. Relatedly, UNDRIP reinforces the foundational principle of self-determination by advocating for Indigenous people's right to FPIC, which is recognised as a vital element for upholding and realising a range of other rights, meaning FPIC is a specific principle that plays a pivotal role in the meaningful application of universally acknowledged human rights related to cultural integrity, equality, and self-determination, particularly for Indigenous people (Mitchell et al., 2019).

It is important to point out that self-determination is a complex and multifaceted concept given it is a polysemic term that is differentially defined both spatially and temporally, particularly by Indigenous communities (Daigel, 2016). Moreover, international law, even when affirming ostensibly 'good' and seemingly progressive rights, inherently legitimates Western liberal governance, entrenches the modern nation state, and is incapable of fully securing self-determination 'from below' (Schilling-Vacaflor and Flemmer, 2020). Critical voices here convincingly argue these dynamics tacitly reproduce a colonial politics of recognition for Indigenous people, which many resolutely and rightly oppose (Coulthard, 2014; Simpson, 2007).

To situate FPIC in the Caribbean, while it has been recognised in international law by the ILO since at least 1989, Belize remains a non-signatory of Convention 169. However, the Belizean government did participate in discussions that led to the creation of both UNDRIP and ADRIP, and it has since subscribed to both. Despite this, the state's purported commitments to FPIC have had minimal impact on the government's relationship with Indigenous groups given its notorious track record of grabbing ancestral lands, sponsoring both extractive and conservation-driven dispossession, and openly – and recurrently – violating both the consent protocol and communal land rights in general (Toledo Anonymous Collective et al., 2022).

It is imperative here to recognise the intrinsic connection between *consultation* and the rights-based principles of FPIC because the state's duty to consult ensures and enforces the rights of Indigenous people, meaning obtaining consent through consultation acts as a fundamental mechanism to actualise the rights of Indigenous people. It also protects them from abuses of state authority. The obligations for governments to consult communities, then, as stipulated in UNDRIP, encompass both procedural and substantive elements to prevent arbitrary actions and achieve equitable results for all parties (Doyle, 2014).

Procedural obligations include genuine efforts to finalise rights under agreed terms; directing interactions between states (or other bodies) and Indigenous communities; attenuating power asymmetries across technical, political, and economic dimensions; ensuring transparency in assessing social and environmental impacts; allowing for appropriate timing; and ensuring Indigenous people are able to select their own representatives. Substantive obligations conversely involve preventing and mitigating negative impacts; setting out fair parameters for compensation and benefit sharing; arranging joint management and monitoring; and establishing proper channels for grievances and damages. The facts on the ground regarding these obligations reveal that 'good faith' adherence to FPIC – a fundamental element of Indigenous people's right to self-determination – is never guaranteed (see Figure 24).

FPIC as Protection and Empowerment or Coercion and Imposition?

With respect to Belize, the formal protocol of FPIC, at least in an official juridical sense, is a relatively new legal practice. When it comes to consultation and consent in Belize, the MLA's standpoint is that FPIC is a foundational principle that should direct all formal dealings between Indigenous groups, state officials, external actors, and third parties. Put succinctly, states, including the government of Belize, must abide by the duty to consult Indigenous people in meaningful and transparent ways. The simple fact that remains all too clear, however, is that what a respective government professes and signs on to at the international and national levels regarding human rights standards and accords is often much different than what it does and how it behaves on the local level.

To date, and despite the 2015 CCJ compliance order requiring the state to collaboratively develop and implement a FPIC protocol alongside the MLA, TAA, and Maya communities, Belize still does not have an official FPIC process. For context, the CCJ ruling, over which the court retains jurisdiction, requires the government of Belize to consult and work in good faith with Maya communities, specifically the appellants, the MLA and TAA, to delimit, demarcate, and title traditional Maya lands. Here, it is paramount that consultation not be approached as a series of isolated, one-time events organised solely on the terms of governments and third parties, which often pit community members against each other (Schilling-Vacaflor and Eichler, 2017). Rather, consultation must be an open

Figure 24 Community mappers discuss logistical plans related to the auto-delimitation of Maya communal lands, which is a core aspect of their practice of self-determination.

Credit: Roberto Kus, Maya Leaders Alliance

iterative dialogue and continuous evolving relationship that pays heed to the temporal, linguistic, and processual preferences of Indigenous communities.

Regarding the Maya case in Belize, one of the first implementation steps the CCJ directed the state to abide by was a mutually agreed upon FPIC protocol. It was specified this needed to be completed in consultation with the MLA and the TAA, which, at the time of this writing, still has not come to fruition. Tellingly, the

Belizean government has dragged out for nearly an entire decade the implementation process mandated by the CCJ. During this time, *unilateral* FPIC protocol filings by the government that were ultimately rejected have coincided with state-sponsored land grabs. These violations continue to result in additional court rulings against the state for its ceaseless disregard for communal land rights and destruction of Maya farmlands and *milpas* (Penados et al., 2021).

A point of contention for the state is the role of the TAA, which it refuses to acknowledge as an Indigenous institution and critical element of customary Maya governance. In fact, the government has openly disavowed the legitimacy of the *alcaldes* and the TAA, and has cast suspicion on Maya communal governance by issuing a statement explicitly asserting: 'We do not believe that there is such a collective governance system of the Maya people.' For Maya of communities across the south, the proximate and long-term detrimental impacts of the government's refusal to agree upon and obtain consent when granting concessions related to 'development' are widespread. Equally, the reprisals the state metes out against Maya villagers and activists who are engaged in organising and land defence does nothing but add more salt into the wound and fuel to the fire.

Environmentally, industrial extraction by logging companies has resulted in the blockage and contamination of waterways, disruptions in Maya harvesting and hunting patterns, and the destruction of agroecological *milpas* as a result of forests that were cleared to open new roads. Natural ecosystems that sustain Maya villages, foodways, and medicinal and healing practices, which are indissoluble from their cultural heritage, have also been disordered, polluted, and marred in ways that are sometimes visibly dramatic and shocking, but in other instances, seemingly go unnoticed by the general public and wider world. For land-based peoples and agrarian societies in affected areas like the Maya of southern Belize, FPIC violations are as detrimental to bioregional ecosystems as they are social relations and spiritual well-being (Leydet, 2019).

Dating back decades, deleterious impacts of state-led neoliberal development for the Maya accrue, compound, and reverberate far beyond the short term, yet are often overlooked. What started with ostensibly simple violations of FPIC that seemingly appeared to have only mild impacts on the Maya people in the immediate moment led to profound damage and a protracted struggle that has gone on for more than thirty years. During that time, FPIC violations, ecological harm, heritage loss, and attempted land/resource grabs have been constant (Penados, 2019).

Furthermore, dragging rural farmers and grassroots organisers from remote hinterlands into and through state courts in distant urban settings and city centres is time-consuming. It requires an immeasurable amount of emotional and intellectual energy, not to mention demands a massive amount of labour, attention, and money. This is all energy, time, resource, and capacity lost by Maya organisers, activists, community members, and elders who could otherwise be working the land, caring for animals, building community, crafting art, creatively expressing, telling stories, passing down knowledge, or engaging in leisure activities like cooking good food, making music, and laughing while dancing with friends, family, and children – if not just resting and relaxing. Taken together, it is arguable that the chronic exhaustion and fatigue induced by state planning procedures and bad faith consultation processes are forms of slow violence in and of themselves. In this way, FPIC violations are at once acts of deliberate abandonment and direct aggression that may not always be volatile events that capture front-page headlines, but they are indeed acts of oppression nonetheless.

The Fraught Politics, Potentials, and Persistent Coloniality of FPIC

As detailed at the beginning of the section, FPIC is the ostensible right Indigenous people have to refuse or permit development actions that may impact their communities and ancestral lands. As a protocol and principle, it authorises Indigenous communities to negotiate the terms and conditions through which projects that will affect their territories will be developed, initiated, monitored, and assessed (Hanna and Vanclay, 2013). As a human rights standard, FPIC stipulates that Indigenous communities must be able to deliberate free from coercion, manipulation, and intimidation, as well as via their preferred time frames and systems of decision-making (Dunlap, 2018). In short, FPIC is meant to ensure that Indigenous people can grant or withhold consent after being fully and effectively informed ahead of time of what any given project entails.

While FPIC has gained a tremendous amount of international traction with respect to securing rights, mitigating environmental damage, and attenuating deforestation, we contend the protocol might be best thought of as an imperfect tool or even a trap that *only at times and in certain instances* can be used to shield Indigenous groups from development aggression and capitalist violence (Gahman, Greenidge, and Mohamed, 2020). As an instrument for safeguarding against land grabbing and partial aspect of self-determination, FPIC has become a politically loaded and hotly contested protocol that implicitly reconsolidates state power, liberal conceptions of rights, and Western legal systems, which often clash with Indigenous cosmologies and can subvert Indigenous people's governance systems (Leydet, 2019). In many ways, rather than securing relative autonomy for Indigenous groups like the Maya of southern Belize and putting an end to the colonial enterprise, FPIC merely mediates it.

Despite its limitations, the FPIC protocol *has the potential to be* (i.e. nothing is guaranteed) an effective albeit constrictive mechanism of accountability Indigenous communities can employ to defend their territories and livelihoods from development programmes that result in alienated lands and ruined bio-cultural heritage (Virtanen, 2019). In essence, what is at stake in Belize regarding FPIC is Indigenous people's right to – and their own definitions of – self-determination. This is in addition to the health of entire ecosystems and the 'reciprocal materialities' (Larsen, 2016) and cultural–spiritual ties Indigenous communities maintain with the non-human world (see Figure 25). Consequently, the ongoing battles related to FPIC in Belize carry global significance and will ultimately carry both regional and international implications, not to mention continue to give rise to pressing questions about the unabating afterlives of imperialism and 'tipping points' associated with climate injustice (Whyte, 2020).

As stressed from the outset of this Element, colonial logics remain a durable and pervasive component of present-day economic growth agendas, land conflicts, and state-based claims to territorial sovereignty and political legitimacy. The protocol of FPIC responds to the undeniable – yet often obscured or flatly denied – reality that the 'modern' development and planning actions of the state readily have destructive and violent effects. Otherwise, why have it?

Figure 25 Community members in regalia perform a historic deer dance which recounts the story of attempted colonial conquest, Maya resistance, and interdependent land relations.

Credit: Roberto Kus, Maya Leaders Alliance

Put differently, FPIC is necessary because Westphalia-inspired states and extractive corporations, alongside their respective claims to top-down authority and penchants for exploiting the environment and racialised 'others', routinely fail to take seriously and respect the diverse ways of being, worldviews, and *relations* of Indigenous people. Accordingly, FPIC protocols are used to signal a purportedly enlightened position by the state yet continue to allow businesses and conservationists to pay lip service to due diligence and gesture towards behaving responsibly in performative manners all while seizing land.

In the Caribbean, FPIC is framed as a promissory note to Indigenous and other groups that governments, businesses, and well-intentioned NGOs have overcome this coloniality and that local communities shall no longer be deceived and disrespected. The irony which remains is that FPIC's very presence is an incriminating confession by the state and private capital that each inherently exist to dispossess. In reality, FPIC, rather than being an apparatus of empowerment that advances self-determination, is the imposition of a contradictory gatekeeping measure that only tenuously holds development aggression and the driving forces of capital accumulation at bay. Clearly, it is not a particularly effective one, which is convenient boon for both the state and extractive corporations (Ødegaard and Rivera Andía, 2019).

Globally, FPIC continues to be framed as a kind of pledge to Indigenous communities that they will no longer be targeted or taken advantage of – that they will be recognised, valued, and afforded the opportunity to determine the nature of their relationship with governments via transparent consultation and consent. The extent to which this is the case, however, is called into question in the realisation that the state is the guarantor of FPIC, meaning that Indigenous communities are forced to engage with the double-edged protocol on the terms and conditions of hierarchical governments. In Belize, state agencies and powerful business interests have used FPIC to mask their dispossessive intentions and violate the duty to consult whilst claiming plausible deniability when acting in bad faith. From grounded Indigenous struggles and grassroots Maya experiences, such violations represent enduring forms of land theft and unrelenting coloniality.

A Five-Point Critical Assessment and Anti-colonial Reflection on FPIC

In reflecting upon the combustible FPIC clashes detailed throughout this Element and the broader environmental politics at hand, we have summarised and next provide five key takeaways and anti-colonial reflections for readers, researchers, and organisers.

Firstly, Indigenous self-determination and practices of kinship, community, and collective governance – as well as approaches to peace, diplomacy, boundaries, and relationships with ecosystems – are heterogeneous and precede colonial contact. All have been alive for generations on end and carry on across a wide array of differing geographies, just as their ancestral memories do. These ever-evolving participatory forms of governance and environmental relations continue to be adversely influenced, affected, and denied by differing (post) colonial institutions and state authorities across the Global South and North, including the government of Belize. Nevertheless, in Toledo District, an Indigenous system of community-based governance remains – the *alcaldes* – which has the TAA as its representative body. It is a direct product of collective consensus, democratic process, and the Maya communities' political agency and territorial relations.

Secondly, states across Central America and the Caribbean like Belize frequently mobilise discourses of economic development, nationalism, and even empowerment to fracture and debilitate Indigenous communities (Navas, Mingorria, and Aguilar-González, 2018). In this case, the government has deployed appeals to nationalism to frame the Maya as recalcitrant and irrational as a means of pitting the wider Belizean population against them. Government administrators have also used liberal–bourgeois conceptions of 'inclusion' and 'authenticity' to discredit and disrupt Indigenous forms of communal governance (e.g. the TAA), organising, and unity. In Belize, this is a foreclosure of self-determination for the Maya communities. Consequently, rural Maya villages can more easily be subjected to misinformation, manipulation, coercion, intimidation, and pressure to acquiesce or accept state-sponsored development projects and actions that negatively affect Maya people, culture, and the environment at large. This is as discomfiting as it is threatening given the Belizean government has a well-documented history of expropriating land and damaging ecosystems.

Thirdly, the historical ongoing tactics, strategies, and policies of contrasting empires and colonial administrators have been to deliberately divide and rule Indigenous communities and sow seeds of internal discord. These splintering processes continue in the contemporary moment in Belize, albeit in a different postcolonial form. This is evidenced by the state-sanctioned dispossession of Indigenous lands and authoritarian nationalism exhibited by the Belizean government, not to mention the bribes and corruption *alcaldes* discussed in Section 3. On this point, it is well worth remembering that the government of Belize is a hierarchical institution of concentrated power that was imposed by the British Empire and remains based upon the Westminster model, meaning formal governance in Belize is just one indicator of how deeply embedded and entrenched colonial institutions, worldviews, and class relations remain across Belize, as well as the Caribbean and Commonwealth. For us, like so many others concerned with collective liberation, freedom comes neither from state policy nor from the well-meaning efforts of NGOs (Thunder Hawk, 2007), but from collective organising, grassroots praxis, and territorial struggle 'from below'.

Fourthly, in considering what FPIC does and means for both Indigenous communities and national governments, it must be reiterated that it is not uncommon for states to agree to human rights accords and FPIC obligations on paper on the global stage, but egregiously violate those accords and obligations behind the scenes locally. In other words, the violent exercise of power to dispossess Indigenous people and prolong their colonial encounter is sanitised, made more subtle, and made invisible or greenwashed through FPIC. When placing the fraught politics of the protocol in Belize under the microscope, it is patently obvious that the government's rap sheet of negligence and retaliation pertaining to FPIC and Indigenous resistance ought neither be minimised as isolated incidents nor framed as mere violations – it is violence. And it is violence, although sometimes 'slow' and oft-concealed, emanating from the 'Master's House' (Lorde, 2018), which is being perpetrated by a postcolonial state performing the most paradoxical type of post-independence belligerence.

Lastly, Indigenous communities are neither uniform nor monolithic. They are characterised by diversity with respect to individual ambitions, core values, customary practices, political ideals, spiritual beliefs, environmental relations, day-to-day opinions, and class divisions across the board (Peller, Penados, and Wainwright, 2023). At times, select members of communities may sell out and side with the aims and agendas of the state, or with the interests and initiatives of corporate extractors, big businesses, and philanthropic conservationists. Similarly, some may even accept 'prestigious' roles as highly paid representatives of governments, corporations, and international NGOs that are engaged in the enclosure, expropriation, and alienation of Indigenous lands and territories. Indeed, as this conflict in Belize demonstrates all too clearly, while the complexion of postcolonial governments and faces of institutions may change – and appear 'native' – the authoritarianism of the state, aggression of 'development', and repression of Indigenous ways of being remain. Even so and equally, Maya environmental defenders in southern Belize are continuing to fight for their relationships with territory, customary governance system, and practice of community in the face of the lasting legacies of colonialism and violence of disavowal – come what may.

8 The Costs, Consequences, and Courage of Resistance

To paint a picture of the local realities of defending territory, community, and relations, this penultimate section is a multi-part compilation of several in-depth interviews with Maya activists who favoured sharing their thoughts on frontline resistance via a joint narrative. The section was composed by the authors, then returned to interviewees for edits and approval. Each subsection addresses questions and direct answers related to the personal and collective challenges organisers face and the costs and consequences of environmental defence.

The Toll Resistance Takes: The Realities of Environmental Defence

Question: In thinking about colonial legacies and the ways the government and third parties define development and growth, can you give us a sense of the realities of environmental defence, as well as discuss the toll resistance takes and how you cope with it all?

As Indigenous community organisers, we are all too familiar with the negative impacts that 'modern development' exerts on our lands, relations, and ways of being. The dominant form of development the government promotes prioritises economic growth and efficiency at the expense of equality, care, and environmental stewardship. It often results in the arrival of large corporations seeking to capitalise on the natural resources of the land, without acknowledging the ecological or cultural harm their activities cause. Our forests, for example, provide us with food, medicine, material for our homes, emotional comfort, and spiritual connection. They are in danger of being severely damaged and stripped bare. This not only injures the Earth but severs us from our ancestral practices and threatens our subsistence and livelihood strategies. I can't emphasise enough how polluting and threatening the forests and waters threatens our dignity.

When you ask about colonialism, I can't help but think of how such legacies continue to loom large over our communities. In many ways, the government and third-party actors still treat our lands as *terra nullius* – empty lands that are free for the taking. This is something Indigenous people face all over the world. That type of mindset dismisses our rooted connections to the land, as well as ignores the sustainable land management practices that our people have developed and passed down for generations – for centuries. These types of colonial outlooks pave the way for 'development' projects that are implemented without our involvement or consent. It leads to a massive amount of damage to the environment, our culture, and our Maya identity. The disrespect shown towards our sacred heritage sites and cultural landmarks are not simple instances of ecological harm, but also a form of erasure. Treating the land like merchandise, raw material, or a cash grab disrupts the transmission of our ancestral knowledge and the customs that have sustained us as *aj ral ch'och'* ('children of the Earth') for generations.

The extractive nature of many industrial practices further compounds the challenges we face and pains we experience. Industries focusing on resource extraction like mining, logging, and oil drilling are conducted with the primary goal of taking as much from the land as possible, as quickly as possible, with little to no regard for long-term consequences. The aftermath is visible in contaminated waterways, polluted air, and deforestation. This environmental degradation disrupts our traditional agroforestry, hunting, fishing, and gathering practices. It also introduces health risks that affect our communities, particularly young people and elders. The loss of biodiversity is not just a loss of plants and animals; it represents a loss of identity and a breakdown of the relations that define us as Maya people. The role of government in these processes compounds the problem. When state authorities align themselves with businesses, the balance of power is tipped against us. You see this for Indigenous communities all over the world. Projects are frequently greenlit without proper consultation, let alone obtaining consent.

In response to these overwhelming challenges, our communities have mobilised to defend our rights and protect our lands and relations (see Figure 26). We have engaged in legal battles to assert our land claims, formed coalitions with

Figure 26 Village members discuss the land rights conflict at an *ab'ink* before a *fahina*, the collective work of maintaining and defending community relations and the commons.

Credit: Roberto Kus, Maya Leaders Alliance

environmental and human rights organisations to amplify our voices, and used new technologies to map our lands and document violations of FPIC as a way to garner international support. We also continue to strengthen our customary governance system, the *alcalde*s, to ensure that our community stands united and strong in the face of external pressure. These efforts are crucial for the survival of Mother Earth, as well as the preservation of our heritage and the integrity of our community relations and traditions.

Our efforts to advocate for our rights and defend the environment are often met with opposition, and in some cases, aggression. There is a lack of accountability on the part of both the government and third parties who are ruining the local environment. When we resist or protest such developments, we are vilified, criminalised, and face harsh repercussions. When the government asserts its power over our communities, it not only is trying to silence our voices but also threatening our physical safety and freedom.

As Maya organisers, advocates, and activists who are on the frontlines, the roles we play in resistance comes with a great deal of risk, danger, and heavy burdens. These are material and emotional and psychological. Very few of us actually call ourselves 'environmental or land defenders', but that is not an incorrect way to think about what we are doing. For many of us, it is not uncommon to experience a palpable feeling of threat. It is not just about the stress of organising protests or negotiating with authorities either. It is about living with the reality that we can be arbitrarily detained, arrested, tossed in jail, and have to live with the fact that we are going to be smeared and misrepresented in local and national media. Such twistings of who we are and what we are doing portrays us as lawbreakers and agitators who do not want to be a part of Belize, which skews public perception and leads to stigma.

Dealing with this type of demonisation day in and day out takes a serious toll on one's mental health. Sometimes the cycle of stress and anxiety is hard to escape. On one level, there is the constant worry about legal ramifications. Each stand we take against developers and the government comes with risk of arrest, criminal charges, and slander. Being criminalised in this way isn't just a risk to our own individual freedom either – it threatens our ability to be there for our families and our communities. The fear of being jailed and the potential for long-and-drawn-out legal battles can be exhausting and paralysing. It puts a strain on accomplishing some of the most basic daily activities.

Beyond the personal legal risks, there is also ridicule and hostility. Our visibility as activists often makes us targets for public scorn, not just in the media, but also in our day-to-day interactions. Getting groceries, going to community meetings, and even attending school events with our kids can turn into nerve-racking situations where we and our families are met with spiteful comments or even outright anger.

This relentless scrutiny adds additional layers of stress, making even simple outings difficult for us and our kids, who also experience anxiety.

This resentment sometimes goes beyond verbal attacks too. There have been instances where property has been vandalised or threats have been made – these are clear messages meant to intimidate and silence us. While we do not back down or let it break our spirit, it does give rise to a certain amount of fear and feelings of vulnerability, even when we are home with our families, which is where you are supposed to feel safest. The thought of our children or loved ones being accosted, bullied, or attacked because of our roles fills me with dread. Their safety and well-being are the most important things. Every aggression and hostile incident is a reminder of the risks we and our families face because of our involvement in the struggle.

Amidst the external threats, the struggle continues. The cumulative effects of ongoing stress, anxiety, and fear can be draining and absolutely take a toll. Sleepless nights filled with unease and a restless mind that cannot escape cycles of worry are common. The physical symptoms of stress, like headaches and fatigue, sometimes seem constant, making it hard to focus or maintain energy for the necessary work of doing community outreach and safeguarding land. I know some who do not really eat for days because of nausea and a couple people who mentioned losing their hair.

Despite these challenges, stepping back is not an option we consider. The connection we have to the land and our duty to protect it are ingrained in us. That said, maintaining mental health is critical. Seeking support from within the community, sharing burdens with those who understand, and reaching out to trusted elders and community members who are supportive are all ways we cope with the stress and manage the pressure. If one thing is certain, it is that the amount of care and conviction we have for each other and our ways of being and lands is greater than any threat posed by the state or rich corporation (see Figure 27).

Protesting Empire, Fortress Conservation, and a British Royal Tour

Question: One major incident that recently captured international headlines was when Maya activists from a village in Toledo protested a British royal visit, which was also related to the specific presence of the Duke and Duchess. Can you give us an overview of what prompted the protest, what it entailed, and the result, fallout, and consequences?

The protest in Indian Creek, a Q'eqchi' Maya village, is an instructive one. It captures several ongoing issues related to land rights, conservation, and consent. For context, it is important to note that Indian Creek was involved in the 2015 CCJ decision that upheld Maya customary land tenure as constitutionally

Figure 27 Maya community members of all ages gather for an *ab'ink*, where they discuss village matters and join their words and thoughts to defend Maya lands.

Credit: Roberto Kus, Maya Leaders Alliance

protected communal property. That historic ruling imposed a legal duty on the government to formalise an FPIC protocol and safeguard Maya lands from encroachment, whether it by the state itself or by third parties.

Despite the ruling, in a troubling development in late 2021, Flora and Fauna International (FFI), an international conservation NGO, was allowed to buy more than 12,000 acres of land traditionally used and enjoyed by Maya community members and farmers from the village. The purchase was sanctioned by the government but conducted without the consent or even consultation of the community. Afterwards, FFI made the situation worse by sending privately hired rangers out to secure and police the area. This effectively barred us from accessing our traditional lands and led to significant disruptions in the village. The hired guards prohibited community members from planting and harvesting, which is central for our food security, health, and culture.

As local Maya villagers, we felt a deep sense of injustice when we learned that the land we have traditionally used for our livelihoods was declared private property owned by FFI, which is supported by members of the British royal family as patrons. This designation prevented us from being on our land, which again, is a vital source of our sustenance and culture. The situation worsened when news broke – not from any direct communication – that the Duke and

Duchess were planning to visit our village as part of their tour of the Caribbean. The royal couple intended to use a local football field as a helicopter landing site for their arrival. Our leaders received word from the government that we needed to 'clean up the village' because we were to receive 'special guests'. This was especially aggravating because all of this was done without our consent. It undermined our rights and the principle of FPIC, which is important to say is not just a formality. [The] FPIC mechanism is there to safeguard our rights and is recognised legally. There is a protocol to follow when it comes to contacting and accessing the village. Things would not have been as bad had that even been respected. The whole thing was also insulting because they assumed the village was dirty and needed to be 'cleaned up'.

In response, the community decided to protest. Leading up to it, though, the situation got intense when the head of police caught wind of our organising and came to the village to warn us about the consequences of protesting the prince's visit. He told us there would be 'repercussions' if we did. This was a clear attempt to intimidate us into backing down. Our intention was to protest when the royals actually landed in their helicopter and were in the village, but we had to go back [to] the drawing board because we found out that no one would be allowed within 200 metres of the football field where they were going to be. We felt we would not be able to send our message as powerfully as we wanted if that were the case. It is our village, but police and soldiers were going to block us. Due to this, we decided to hold our protest on Friday, before the weekend, to capture as much media attention as possible. So we organised, made signs, and collectively protested.

Our demonstration ended up forcing the Duke and Duchess to cancel their visit to a cacao farm in Indian Creek, which had been planned as the first stop on their Caribbean tour. It was intense and rubbed a few people the wrong way because following our protest, a smaller counterprotest was organised by individuals more sympathetic to the British monarchy and [the] government's wish to showcase Maya 'entrepreneurialism'. This created tension in the village. The counterprotest, unlike ours, which was aimed at broad community issues including land rights and even colonialism, was, in my opinion, more personal in nature and tied to the government's interests. I get that the royal tour was meant to strengthen ties and garner support for the royals, but for us, it seemed like a cheap attempt at a photo op and like we would be used as props and tokens. It was a reminder of the way colonial masters behaved and highlighted ongoing issues related to how the Maya people's land rights and desire for self-determination are ignored.

Representatives from FFI later stated that they had purchased the land from private owners with the goal of conserving wildlife while supporting the livelihoods and traditional rights of local communities like ours. I think they do this by working through a local NGO but not the grassroots movement. They (FFI) pledged to maintain an open dialogue, yet this promise felt hollow because it is not happening in practice and they have already caused a great deal of disruption and [a] tremendous amount of distress amongst the community. The involvement of high-profile patrons of FFI, in particular the royals, reveals how conservation efforts, which, in cases like Indian Creek, are given priority and seen as more important than the rights and customary land uses of Indigenous communities. This is a form of 'fortress conservation' and has been criticised by the UN's Special Rapporteur on Indigenous Peoples because it contravenes human rights principles, particularly those concerning Indigenous peoples' rights to self-determination, access to natural resources, and FPIC.

Ironically, I think the way Maya people manage the forest also conserves it, and the approach taken by FFI is just a form of greenwashing. By purchasing large swathes for conservation, the NGO claims to preserve the environment, but, in reality, it is dispossessing the Maya and banning local farmers from accessing land. It is a disturbing trend all over the world and the well-meaning efforts of conservation NGOs and the Duke and Duchess are in no way correcting historical wrongs. The government (of Belize) and police are not helping either.

The government argues the land in question is national and can be sold legally to third parties without the consent of Maya community members. This view clearly contradicts the stipulations of the 2015 CCJ consent order that you know about, which mandates that the state refrain from actions that would adversely affect Maya communities' uses and enjoyments of their lands until a proper mechanism is established to recognise and protect our lands. Overall, the protest in Indian Creek highlights the urgent need for the Belize government to engage in good faith and respect and enforce the customary practices of the Maya people, as well as ensure that third parties are also complying with legal and ethical obligations. Both international and domestic frameworks support this and emphasise the necessity of upholding the dignity, rights, and survival of Indigenous communities and cultures against so-called modern conservation efforts and governmental interests.

I want to stress that the situation at Indian Creek involving FFI and the royal family is not just a local issue or single incident either. It is a clear illustration of the wider legacies of empire and colonialism. These are legacies of land grabbing and belittling Indigenous people that should not be celebrated. Other groups protested too, as I know there were incidents in Jamaica and calls for an apology in the Bahamas. This type of behaviour can be seen in a variety of different present-day conservation and philanthropy efforts. It is happening to Indigenous groups all over Africa. In many cases, conservation projects are nothing other than fronts for land grabs. Our protest of the royals and FFI here in Belize was a textbook case of how colonial history and power dynamics can be seen in the present.

In terms of the consequences of speaking out against the royal visit and FFI, we protestors faced a great deal of backlash. We were portrayed as divisive and irrational troublemakers who are anti-development and greedy in the media and by state officials. This made things worse, caused tensions to rise, and tempers to flare. It was stressful and took a massive emotional toll that did not just go away after a couple of days too. Speaking against powerful entities like governments and international NGOs like FFI, which have far more resources at their disposal than we do, can feel like a bit of a David-versus-Goliath scenario. Protesters faced character assassination, their motives were questioned, and their names were smeared. Such stereotypes can be alienating and make us targets. Meanwhile, organisations like FFI can just ignore it, wait, and hope it goes away.

Even weeks after the demonstration, I was falsely accused of assault by the police and jailed over a weekend. It was timed so there would be no government offices open to process my release until the next Monday. The timing was not a coincidence – it was a deliberate attempt to make me feel isolated and send a message. One officer admitted the arrest was because of the protest. It was not about justice being served because I did not do anything or attack anyone; it was a clear abuse of authority meant to silence and punish me.

Over the past year, incidents like this have happened three times. I have been taken in by the police on multiple occasions but never formally charged for anything. Repeated episodes like this are meant to break our spirit and deter us from being involved in community advocacy and protest actions. After it kept happening, I realised the importance of addressing the matter in a more official manner and sought support from local councillors, which has helped curb the harassment. Despite all the hardships, we keep going. It is not just about one person either. It is not about having a big name or personal gain; we are doing this for the community, for our people, and for our children – and their children.

9 Indigenous Future-Making: Defending and Making Life

This concluding section is fittingly written by Filiberto, who has walked between the worlds of academia and the Maya struggle for decades. In addition to drawing from more than twenty years of engaged praxis and critical observations related to community organising, autonomous education, and movement building in Belize and beyond, it includes invaluable insights about the realities of the Maya people from an initiative he led with communities entitled 'The Future We Dream'. Throughout the reflection, Filiberto also draws upon decolonial scholarship and stories he heard as a child to illustrate the ways in which Indigenous struggles for land and freedom are connected across histories, memories, geographies, and generations.

Figure 28 *Yax'che'*, the *ceiba* tree, is the tree of life and carries deep cultural and spiritual significance for communities. It symbolises Maya relationships with the cosmos and ancestors.

Credit: Roberto Kus, Maya Leaders Alliance

'The Future We Dream' Initiative: Envisioning Alternative Worlds

The Maya struggle to defend territory, community, and relations is a battle for the future that is rooted in ancestral memory (see Figure 28) – not to mention what it means to be human. While defending and affirming Maya rights to land has a centuries-long history, the current iteration, as outlined earlier, dates back to the 1990s when the government of Belize unilaterally granted access to ancestral Maya lands by issuing logging concessions to a multinational corporation. The extractivist encroachments were justified via the notorious and all too familiar *terra nullius* ('empty land') myth, which the Belizean state continues to deploy to facilitate land grabs and abuses of both nature and labour. In short, what the Maya communities of southern Belize are 'non-metaphorically' confronting as Indigenous people are the systemic practices of erasure, elimination, exploitation, and dispossession that define colonial–capitalist modernity (Tuck and Yang, 2012).

For generations, the Maya's presence on their ancestral lands has been deemed invisible, illicit, and insufficient. Via the legal system, the government has argued that while the Maya may be Indigenous, they are not indigenous to Belize, and furthermore, that whatever rights the Maya might have had at one time were later extinguished through colonial dispossession and the process of post-independence nation-building that followed. In this way, the postcolonial state is seeking to evict and erase Maya people, culture, and connections to the land, which is a reality for other Indigenous people in the Caribbean (Jackson, 2012).

More recently, neoliberal notions of 'development' and 'growth' have been used to frame Q'eqchi' and Mopan communities as backward, unreasonable, stolid, selfish, torpid, and divisive. These are by no means new racist charges levelled against Indigenous communities given they went global in 1492. The current position of the government reflects the operation of the 'coloniality of power', which perpetuates ongoing dispossession through erasure, condemnation, and expulsion (Quijano, 2000). Against this, the Maya movement has counterposed their long-standing use, occupation, and enjoyments of their ancestral territories – as well as their sustained ways of being and relations with land – around collective ownership, complex tenure, and communal stewardship, not as something of the past, but of the future.

In this way, the Maya communities are practising and advancing Indigenous future-making, which is perhaps most readily evident in a 2018 initiative they undertook titled 'The Future We Dream'. This collective visioning project, which prioritised inclusive and participatory processes, saw the Maya communities engage in reflection and dialogue about their shared identity, realities, desired futures, and alternative 'worlds', as the Zapatistas might say. Representatives from a cross-section of Maya communities in southern Belize participated in a series of Maya dreaming *ab'inks* (community assemblies).

Using the practice of *ab'ink* and arts-based methods, they answered three basic questions: (1) Who are we as Maya people? (2) What are our pains and joys? (3) What are our dreams for the future of our land and our people? The reflections and drawings they shared offered powerful insights into Maya future imaginaries. Images of Maya dress, temples, collective work, life in the community, life on the land, the fruitfulness of the land, spiritual ceremony, local foods, and Maya languages were used to epitomise who they are. Participants represented themselves as people with their own identity, history, and ways of knowing and doing. They characterised themselves as a people with a long history on their land, with a clear path from ancestral ancient temples to present-day Maya thatch-roofed huts.

Across the *ab'inks*, participants asserted themselves as people of the land. Their reflections about territory, forests, rivers, water, and environmental relations poignantly communicated the concept of *aj ral ch'och'* (being 'children of the Earth') as elemental to being – to Maya existence. Being *aj ral ch'och'* is to depend upon, live on, work, and take care of the land. The reflections remind me of the Mopan and

Yucatec concept of *yokol cab*, the term for Earth, which literally translates on 'top of honey'. The land was clearly represented as the source of this rich, nourishing, and healing substance for both the Maya and other beings. The nourishment of the land is the result of a reciprocal relationship with the land and each other.

Life on the land and caring for the land is not a mere individual, instrumental, and unidirectional relationship – nor is it simply material. Participant illustrations of the collective construction of thatch-roofed houses and planting of corn in *milpa*s were reminders that it takes a community to achieve well-being and sustain reciprocal relationships with the land. The message that to be *aj ral cho'ch'* is to be in community was made clearer through their use of terms such as *junajil* (unity) and *komonil* (oneness). Drawings of mountains, hills, and valleys – of caves and of Maya people making offerings – were also reminders that the *Tzul Taka*, 'the lord of the hills and mountains', is the true owner and protector of the land, forest, animals, and plants – a reminder of the spiritual dimension of Maya land relations.

Through their collective visioning and discussions related to alternative realities/worlds, the Maya participants in 'The Future We Dream' project were rescuing their *being* from colonial logics. That they were doing so was made evident by one of the groups who offered a stark and contrasting representation of how the Maya people are viewed and stigmatised by the state and some members of civil society. They drew a person draped in the Belizean flag with a thought bubble. In the thought bubble, the Maya were epitomised by an emaciated person holding out a begging bowl who was next to an equally gaunt and mangy dog, alongside an unkempt person lying on the ground who was drunk and surrounded by dirt and flies. The drawing underscored the contemptuous racialism and coloniality of the state, as well as reflected the political agency and decolonial subjectivity of the Maya participants who were critically reading the (ongoing colonial) world around them.

Emancipatory Visions of Sustainable and Socially Just Futures

The Maya participants' visions of the future spoke to a variety of themes: rootedness to territory and community, autonomy, dignity, land security, the interconnected well-being of the human and non-human worlds, and even respectful relationships with the state. The drawings of Maya futures too depicted life on the land, food sovereignty, collective work, agroforestry, Maya dress, thriving languages, life in community, and a clear message that the future is rooted in Maya ways of being, knowing, and doing. The drawings included schools, clinics, improved roads, new technologies, alternative economic activities, positive interactions with ministry officials, demarcated lands, and laws that protect Maya lands – in short, new routes. In their dreamed-of futures, the Maya further imagined respectful relationships with the government. In one of their drawings, two people shaking hands were featured. One person is dressed in a red suit jacket while the other has a bag hanging from their shoulder. There is no mistaking the fact that the person with the bag is a Maya leader, an *alcalde*, who is carrying their *coxtal* (sling bag), as is common across Toledo District. The person in the red jacket is a government representative given red was the colour representing the political party in power at the time. Clearly, the Maya dream of the future requires a transformation of the state.

A critical element of 'The Future We Dream' was autonomy. On this point and in their illustrations, women were explicit that they dreamed of having a home and land to produce their own local foods, in particular *caldo* (soup). The significance of *caldo* in Maya communities is worth noting here. It is a symbol of well-being, hospitality, conviviality, medicine, reciprocity, and dignity. *Caldo* is also at the centre of communing together, as well as carries spiritual importance. That women specified they want to grow, produce, and control their own local foods and diets communicates the importance of identity, rootedness, nourishing others, food sovereignty, self-sufficiency, and – in a word – autonomy.

The interconnectedness between the well-being of land and people was another prominent theme. The women were direct in envisioning people working together in harmony, supporting one another, and caring for each other. Notably, *junajil* (unity) and *komonil* (oneness) recurrently appeared in drawings across participants and villages, which denotes just how fundamental being united is for the well-being of both the land and Maya people throughout southern Belize. The health of the land was exemplified by illustrations of clean, flowing rivers, lush forests, colourful fruitfulness, and even monkeys swinging in trees, which signalled a desire for non-human life to be present, coexist, and thrive on the land. In one drawing, well-being was represented as a 'happy family village'. In Q'eqchi terms, this desire is referred to as *usilal*, which translates to goodness–happiness. It means people have secure land, plentiful food, meaningful work, dignity, and freedom (see Figure 29).

Throughout the process, participant drawings indicated they wanted accessible and quality education which is distinctively culturally safe. Drawings depicted a classroom where the title of the lesson was *qatinob'aal* ('our language') and the school itself was labelled *tz'olebaal* (a Maya place of learning). The use of the Q'eqchi language was intentional to communicate that the education participants envisioned is defined by the Maya communities – an education that confronts the 'coloniality of being' to make space for Maya knowledges, languages, and cultural practices (Maldonado-Torres, 2007). In an even more explicit drawing related to autonomy, a welcome sign to a community reads: 'Welcome to Maya

Figure 29 Village members from all ages walk and converse in a Maya forest garden, a reminder of environmental relations and what it means to live well on the land as a community.

Credit: Roberto Kus, Maya Leaders Alliance

people's lands', which include buildings designated as *Maya* schools, hospitals, and even banks. Clearly, community members are dreaming of self-defined and autonomous schools, clinics, and banks anchored in Maya ways of being.

Several drawings of the future also included new technologies, infrastructure, and alternative economic activities integrated into existing Maya relations and customs: a solar panel on a thatch roof, a room with books in one corner and traditional medicine in the other, a Maya home with rooms to offer to others, a music school teaching traditional music, agroecological systems producing cacao, corn, and other local crops, and solar energy fields providing the community with energy. The economic activities depicted made use of both the Maya's cultural and natural heritage in new contexts. These aspects of the drawings were consistently balanced to communicate that Maya ways of being and notions of community are inextricably linked to healthy relationships with the land.

Markedly, the dream of the future of the Maya is neither about going back to some idealised static past, nor is it about closing Maya communities off to other cultural horizons. It is a desire for *re-rooting* and *rerouting* their knowledge, culture, and relations. It is about finding routes that both sustain and allow for *aj ral cho'ch'* to be continually recreated. In a summative vision statement, the Maya participants collectively declared:

> We are peaceful, hardworking, self-determining people open to the world and new technologies living in community and collectively stewarding the well-being of our people and our lands.

The fundamental element of this vision is the stewardship of well-being of land and people – made possible by peacefulness, autonomy, community, and openness. The Maya's 'The Future We Dream' exercise was put in the service of both unshackling their communities from imperial modes of living and opening a decolonial dreaming space.

Against a backdrop of ongoing colonial worldviews and neoliberal developmentalism that frame Indigenous people as broken, docile, and deficient, the Maya asserted their Maya-ness by posing the query: 'Who are we as Maya people?' The process of answering this very question affirmed Maya ways of being by confronting the dehumanisation they continue to face under the spectre of coloniality, the capitalist world system, and the post-independent Westminster-modelled state. Overall, in the face of the domesticating, disciplinary, and 'straightening' (Ahmed, 2007) technologies of economic growth agendas bourgeois respectability politics that are part and parcel of Western-liberal modernity, the Maya envisioning process was a subversive act of resistance and emancipatory *re-rooting* that created a space where Maya ways of knowing, being, and doing – not to mention alternative worlds and futures – could be dreamt of and flourish freely.

Why Are Indigenous Movements and Territorial Struggles Important?

The simple answer to the question as to why Indigenous movements and territorial struggles are important is because they are *hopeful* struggles. In addition to having discourses and theories of decolonisation, they are defined more so by their collective *practice* of decolonisation (Rivera Cusicanqui, 2020). The poly-crisis humanity currently faces highlights the urgent need to imagine, enact, and build better 'worlds'. Amidst myriad impending global catastrophes, Indigenous communities and grassroots movements 'from below' are leading the way (Cox, Nilsen, and Pleyers, 2017). They are dreaming and crafting alternative futures that can equally teach and inspire.

On this point, Quijano (2000) observes: 'What is termed globalization is the culmination of a process that began with the constitution of America and colonial/modern Eurocentered capitalism as a new global power.' What has been globalised is a particular way of exercising power referred to as modernity – which is liberal-colonial-capitalist – and is referred to by some as racial capitalism (Robinson, 2020). As Grosfoguel notes, this modernity/coloniality was not only economic expansion, the extension of Europe to the rest of the world, or the incorporation of exploited labour from colonised areas into an international division of labour; rather it was the annihilation of other forms of life. Grosfoguel (2018) succinctly summarises this by stating: 'It was the destruction of other civilizations and imposition of a new one.'

This new civilisation – modernity – embodies a way of relating to the land and to each other underpinned by the de-sacralisation of nature, hierarchisation of difference, expendability of negatively racialised bodies, exteriorisation of 'the other', rejection of the past, promotion of competitive rugged individualism, primacy of private property, and extraction of value via the enclosure and extraction of the commons (Federici, 2019). On these matters, Grosfoguel (2018) aptly sums up the links between capitalism and modernity:

> If capitalism is genocidal, epistemicidal, ecocidal, racist, Christian-centric, Eurocentric, sexist, destructive of communities, of the agrarian world, of the peasantry, it is because it is organized from within the civilizing logic of modernity.

It is this life-destructiveness that must be confronted to make possible alternative futures. For the Maya communities in southern Belize, this is precisely what Indigenous future-making (i.e. defending territory, community, and relations) entails.

In thinking about global Indigenous struggles, Dussel (2002, 234) points out that 'there are present-day cultures that predate European modernity, that have developed together with it, and that have survived until the present with enough human potential to give birth to a cultural plurality that will emerge after modernity and capitalism'. From an exteriority that modernity has ignored, relegated, and not been able to subsume, but which existed alongside and developed with modernity, Dussel (2000) argues the project of 'transmodernity' emerges, which is a '"*beyond*" that transcends Western modernity and that will have a creative function of great significance' (Dussel 2002, 221). For Dussel (2000), transmodernity is 'subsuming the best of globalized European and North American modernity', affirming '"from *without*" the essential components of modernity's own excluded cultures', and, from this, developing 'a new civilization for the twenty-first century' (Dussel, 2002).

Indigenous future-making exemplifies transmodernity. Indigenous people are frequently cast as remnants and victims of the past, marginal to the present, as peripheral groups who have very little to contribute, and will therefore likely be unable to make it into the future. On the contrary, as countless Indigenous movements, including the Maya in southern Belize, are demonstrating, Indigenous people are future-makers. In this vein, Roanhorse (2015) contends,

> To be a Native of North America is to exist in a space where the past and the future mix in a delicate swirl of the here-and-now. We stand with one foot always in the darkness that ended our world, and the other in a hope for our future as Indigenous people. It is from this apocalyptic in-between that the Indigenous voices in speculative fiction speak.

Indigenous future-making emphasises the agency and creativity of Indigenous people without recourse to romanticising the past. It moves away from what Tuck (2009) refers to as 'deficit-' and 'damaged-centred' approaches to 'desired-based' standpoints and aspirations. Indigenous future-making further departs from reductive dualisms like 'traditional versus modern' and 'developed versus advanced' as a way to leave colonial–capitalist modernity behind.

In thinking of colonial histories and times past, the notion of Indigenous future-making is neither a call to 'get over it' nor to thoughtlessly 'move on' amidst the open wounds and unresolved traumas owed to colonialism and racial dehumanisation. Far from it. Indigenous future-making involves a 'double vision', a process of re-rooting and rerouting that is perhaps best captured in Humberto Ak'abal's (1996) poem '*Camino al Revés* [Walking Backwards]', which reads:

> Once in a while
> I walk backwards
> It is my way of remembering.
> If I only walked forward
> I would be able to tell you
> what it means to forget.

Indigenous future-making involves turning towards the past, remembering, rediscovering, and reclaiming not as a means of going back, but as a way to reflect upon and be critically guided by the past. It is about recovering the self, knowledge, and Indigenous histories.

In sum, Indigenous future-making confronts the 'coloniality of power' as it seeks to unsettle and undo enduring colonial hierarchies, dichotomies, and binaries, in addition to disentangling and emancipating subjectivities, land, and labour from their subordination to both capital and state power. Indigenous future-making involves the kind 'sustainable self-determination' proposed by Corntassel (2012), as well as various forms of 'resurgence' discussed by other critical Indigenous scholars (Alfred, 2023; Coulthard, 2014; Simpson, 2017). It is precisely the type of 'radical resurgence' that Simpson (2017) calls for – one with a clear commitment to alternative paths, 'worlds otherwise', and a revolutionary reordering of social relations – in addition to radically hopeful and life-giving futures (see Figure 30).

Figure 30 One of many quiet and faintly perceptible forest paths used by Maya villagers, epitomising the ways in which their relations and rhythms of life work with – rather than against – nature.

Credit: Roberto Kus, Maya Leaders Alliance

A Coda on Coloniality, Indigenous Struggles, and Future-Making

Growing up, my mother would say, 'One is not an Indian who does not keep their stone' as a way of describing someone who does not forget a past injury, one could say someone who holds a grudge, though this is often portrayed as a moral flaw. For my mother, however, forgiving did not mean forgetting. In thinking about Indigenous struggles, not forgetting our 'stone' necessitates remaining ever aware of and tending to our colonial injuries, yet persisting in struggle. I think this is part of my mother's teaching. Before she passed away, my mother bequeathed me a different kind of stone – a grinding stone. It was upon the grinding stone that the gods ground the corn to make Maya people.

The grinding stone, in some places, is still used for preparing corn for the tortillas that symbolise life, which, seemingly un-coincidentally, is work done mostly by Maya women. The stone is also connected to planting and harvesting corn, which, for many Maya men, is a reminder of the possibility of escaping exploitative waged labour and finding freedom. The grinding stone is used in new livelihood strategies – crushing the cacao in the chocolate-making experiences that the Maya sell to tourists, for example. The other part of my mother's teaching seems to be that keeping our stone is about holding on to Maya ways of being, heritage, resistance, resilience, well-being, and autonomy, all of which the grinding stone represents. Indeed, Indigenous future-making is about keeping our stone as a shield and weapon to defend life, to sustain life, and to create a future.

Concerns and discussions about the dismal global future, the precipice we are on, often ignore the fact that what we currently are experiencing is the culmination of a process that began some time ago. Dakota scholar Tallbear (2023, 102) puts it concisely:

> Dakota people's apocalyptic grieving has a longer timeline; we are at a different stage of grief. The genocide over hundreds of years of Indigenous peoples in the Americas and the co-decimation of nonhuman relatives and their societies brings us and you to here. It is this world built out of our apocalypse that is now at risk.

Indigenous people's efforts to defend territory, community, and relations – like the struggle for land and self-determination of the Maya in southern Belize – is about imagining and co-creating more just and sustainable futures. This requires transcending capitalist modernity, colonial worldviews, neoliberal logic, and the life-destroying practices that produced a veritable apocalypse for Indigenous people, which is something all of humanity currently faces. Confronting those destructive forces is now everyone's struggle – we cannot afford to forget our stones.

References

Ahmed, S. (2007). A phenomenology of whiteness. *Feminist Theory*, 8(2), 149–168.

Ak'abal, H. (1996). *Ajkem Tz'ij: Tejedor de Palabras*. Guatemala City: Cholsamaj.

Alfred, T. (2023). *It's All about the Land: Collected Talks and Interviews on Indigenous Resurgence*. Toronto: University of Toronto Press.

Altamirano-Jimenez, I. (2013). *Indigenous Encounters with Neoliberalism: Place, Women, and the Environment in Canada and Mexico*. Vancouver: University of British Columbia Press.

Anaya, S. J. (2008). Reparations for neglect of Indigenous land rights at the intersection of domestic and international law: The Maya cases in the Supreme Court of Belize. In F. Lenzerini, ed., *Reparations for Indigenous Peoples: International and Comparative Perspectives*. Oxford: Oxford University Press, pp. 567–603.

Baines, K. (2015). *Embodying Ecological Heritage in a Maya Community: Health, Happiness, and Identity*. Lanham: Lexington Books.

Baines, K., and Zarger, R. (2024). Dilemmas of making and unmaking environmental and cultural heritage in southern Belize. *International Journal of Heritage Studies*, 30(9), 1088–1102. https://doi.org/10.1080/13527258.2024.2369556.

Beckford, G. L. (1972). *Persistent Poverty: Underdevelopment in Plantation Economies of the Third World*. Oxford: Oxford University Press.

Benton, L., and Straumann, B. (2010). Acquiring empire by law: From Roman doctrine to early modern European practice. *Law and History Review*, 28(1), 1–38.

Bolland, O. N. (2003). *Colonialism and Resistance in Belize: Essays in Historical Sociology*. Benque Viejo del Carmen: Cubola Books.

Braaten, D. (2022). A triangle of vulnerability: Global demand for resources, political marginalization, and a culture of impunity as causes of environmental defender killings. *Human Rights Quarterly*, 44(3), 537–563.

Cahill, C., and Pain, R. (2019). Representing slow violence and resistance: On hiding and seeing. *ACME: An International Journal for Critical Geographies*, 18(5), 1054–1065.

Campbell, M. S., and Anaya, S. J. (2008). The case of the Maya villages of Belize: Reversing the trend of government neglect to secure Indigenous land rights. *Human Rights Law Review*, 8(2), 377–399.

Caserta, S. (2018). The contribution of the Caribbean Court of Justice to the development of human and fundamental rights. *Human Rights Law Review*, 18(1), 170–184.

Cordis, S. (2019). Forging relational difference: Racial gendered violence and dispossession in Guyana. *Small Axe: A Caribbean Journal of Criticism*, 23(3), 18–33.

Corntassel, J. (2012). Re-envisioning resurgence: Indigenous pathways to decolonization and sustainable self-determination. *Decolonization: Indigeneity, Education and Society*, 1(1), 86–101.

Coulthard, G. S. (2014). *Red Skin, White Masks: Rejecting the Colonial Politics of Recognition*. Minneapolis: University of Minnesota Press.

Cox, L., Nilsen, A., and Pleyers, G. (2017). Social movement thinking beyond the core: Theories and research in post-colonial and postsocialist societies. *Interface: A Journal for and about Social Movements*, 9(2), 1–36.

Cuestas-Caza J. (2018). *Sumak kawsay* is not *buen vivir*. *Alternautas*, 5(1), 49–63.

Cupples, J., and Grosfoguel, R. (2019). *Unsettling Eurocentrism in the Westernised University*. Abingdon: Routledge.

Daigle, M. (2016). *Awawanenitakik*: The spatial politics of recognition and relational geographies of Indigenous self-determination. *The Canadian Geographer/Le Géographe Canadien*, 60(2), 259–269.

Davis, J., Moulton, A. A., Van Sant, L., and Williams, B. (2019). Anthropocene, capitalocene . . . plantationocene? A manifesto for ecological justice in an age of global crises. *Geography Compass*, 13(5), e12438.

Downey, S. S., Walker, M., Moschler, J., Penados, F., Peterman, W., Pop, J., and Song, S. (2023). An intermediate level of disturbance with customary agricultural practices increases species diversity in Maya community forests in Belize. *Nature Communications Earth & Environment*, 4(1), 1–13. https://doi.org/10.1038/s43247-023-01089-6.

Doyle, C. M. (2014) *Indigenous Peoples, Title to Territory, Rights and Resources: The Transformative Role of Free, Prior, and Informed Consent*. Abingdon: Routledge.

Dunlap, A. (2018). A bureaucratic trap: Free, prior, and informed consent (FPIC) and wind energy development in Juchitán, Mexico. *Capitalism Nature Socialism*, 29(4), 88–108.

Dussel, E. (2000). Europe, modernity, and Eurocentrism. *Nepantla: Views from the South*, 1(3), 465–478.

Dussel, E. (2002). World-system and "trans"-modernity. *Nepantla: Views from the South*, 3(2), 221–244.

Environmental Law Alliance Worldwide (ELAW). (2015). *The Maya Leaders Alliance v. The Attorney General of Belize*. https://cutt.ly/MLAvsBelize.

Fanon, F. (1963). *The Wretched of the Earth*. New York: Grove Press.

Farmer, P. (2004). An anthropology of structural violence. *Current Anthropology*, 45, 305–325.

Federici, S. (2019). *Re-enchanting the World: Feminism and the Politics of the Commons*. San Francisco: PM Press.

Gahman, L. (2020). Contra plantation, prison, and capitalist annihilation: Collective struggle, social reproduction, and the co-creation of lifegiving worlds. *Journal of Peasant Studies*, 47(3), 503–524.

Gahman, L., Greenidge, A., and Mohamed, A. (2020). Plunder via violation of FPIC: Land grabbing, state negligence, and pathways to peace in Central America and the Caribbean. *Journal of Peacebuilding & Development*, 15(3), 372–376.

Gahman, L., Penados, F., and Greenidge, A. (2020). Indigenous resurgence, decolonial praxis, alternative futures: The Maya Leaders Alliance of Southern Belize. *Social Movement Studies*, 19(2), 241–248.

Gahman, L., Penados, F., Greenidge, A., Miss, S., Kus, R., Makin, D., Xuc, F., Kan, R., and Rash, E. (2020). Dignity, dreaming, and desire-based research in the face of slow violence: Indigenous youth organising as (counter)development. *Interface: A Journal for and about Social Movements*, 12(1), 616–651.

Gahman, L., Penados, F., and Smith, S. J. (2023). Environmental defenders and social movements: The violent realities of resisting extractivism. In V. Desai, E. Dauncey, and A. Pinkerton, eds., *The Companion to Development Studies* (4th edition). Abingdon: Routledge, pp. 176–181.

Ghazoul, J., and Kleinschroth, F. (2018). A global perspective is needed to protect environmental defenders. *Nature Ecology & Evolution*, 2(9), 1340–1342.

Global Witness. (2020). *Defending Tomorrow: The Climate Crisis and Threats against Land and Environmental Defenders*. London: Global Witness.

Grandia, L. (2012). *Enclosed: Conservation, Cattle, and Commerce among the Q'eqchi' Maya Lowlanders*. Seattle: University of Washington Press.

Grosfoguel, R. (2018). La compleja relación entre modernidad y capitalismo: Una visión descolonial. *Pléyade (Santiago)*, 21, 29–47.

Guzmán Hormazábal, L. (2019). Worrying rise in deaths of environmental activists. *SciDev.Net*. www.scidev.net/global/governance/news/worrying-rise-in-deaths-of-environmental-activists.html.

Haines, S. (2012). Meaningful resources and resource-full meanings: Spatial and political imaginaries in southern Belize. In M. Janowski and T, Ingold, eds., *Imagining Landscapes: Past, Present and Future*. Burlington: Ashgate, pp. 97–120.

Haines, S. (2018). Imagining the highway: Anticipating infrastructural and environmental change in Belize. *Ethnos*, 83(2), 392–413.

Hanna, P., and Vanclay, F. (2013). Human rights, Indigenous peoples and the concept of Free, Prior and Informed Consent. *Impact Assessment and Project Appraisal*, 31(2), 146–157.

Inter-American Commission on Human Rights (IACHR). (2004). *Maya Indigenous Communities of the Toledo District v Belize*. Report No 40/04, Case 12.053. www.cidh.org/annualrep/2004eng/Belize.12053eng.htm.

Intergovernmental Panel on Climate Change (IPCC). (2022). *Climate Change 2022: Impacts, Adaptation and Vulnerability*. Contribution of Working Group II to the Sixth Assessment Report of the Intergovernmental Panel on Climate Change [H.-O. Pörtner, D. C. Roberts, M. Tignor, E. S. Poloczanska, K. Mintenbeck, A. Alegría, M. Craig, S. Langsdorf, S. Löschke, V. Möller, A. Okem, B. Rama (eds.)]. Cambridge: Cambridge University Press. https://doi.org/10.1017/9781009325844.

Jackson, S. N. (2014). Humanity beyond the regime of labor: Antiblackness, indigeneity, and the legacies of colonialism in the Caribbean. *Decolonization: Indigeneity, Education, and Society*. https://decolonization.wordpress.com/2014/06/06/humanity-beyond-the-regime-of-labor-antiblackness-indigeneity-and-the-legacies-of-colonialism-in-the-Caribbean.

Jackson, S. N. (2012). *Creole Indigeneity: Between Myth and Nation in the Caribbean*. Minneapolis: University of Minnesota Press.

Kus, R., Gahman, L., Greenidge, A., Penados, F., and Smith, S. J. (2023). Snapshots of Maya Self-determination in Southern Belize. *NACLA Report on the Americas*, 55(3), 294–304. https://doi.org/10.1080/10714839.2023.2247761.

Larsen, S. C. (2016). Regions of care: A political ecology of reciprocal materialities. *Journal of Political Ecology*, 23(1), 159–166.

Leifsen, E., Gustafsson, M. T., Guzmán-Gallegos, M. A., and Schilling-Vacaflor, A. (2017). New mechanisms of participation in extractive governance: Between technologies of governance and resistance work. *Third World Quarterly*, 38(5), 1043–1057.

Le Billon, P., and Lujala, P. (2020). Environmental and land defenders: Global patterns and determinants of repression. *Global Environmental Change*, 65, 1–16.

Leydet, D. (2019). The power to consent: Indigenous peoples, states, and development projects. *University of Toronto Law Journal*, 69(3), 371–403.

Liboiron, M. (2021). *Pollution Is Colonialism*. Durham: Duke University Press.

Loperena, C. (2022). *The Ends of Paradise: Race, Extraction, and the Struggle for Black Life in Honduras*. Redwood City: Stanford University Press.

Lorde, A. (2018). *The Master's Tools Will Never Dismantle the Master's House*. London: Penguin UK.

Losurdo, D. (2014). *Liberalism: A Counter-History*. London: Verso Books.

Maldonado-Torres, N. (2007). On the coloniality of being: Contributions to the development of a concept. *Cultural Studies*, 21(2–3), 240–270.

McGee, R., and Pettit, J. (2020). *Power, Empowerment and Social Change*. Abingdon: Routledge.

McGrane, C., Mohamed, N., and Gahman, L. (2023). Gender, environmental conflict, and direct action. In R. Baikady, S. M. Sajid, J. Przeperski, V. Nadesan, M. R. Islam, and J. Gao, eds., *The Palgrave Handbook of Global Social Change*. Cham: Palgrave Macmillan, pp. 1–23.

Menton, M., and Le Billon, P. (eds.). (2021). *Environmental Defenders: Deadly Struggles for Life and Territory*. : Abingdon: Routledge.

Mesh, T. (2017). *Alcaldes* of Toledo, Belize: Their Genealogy, Contestation, and Aspirations. PhD Dissertation, University of Florida.

Miss, S., Kus, R., Penados, F., and Gahman, L. (2021). Joy against the machine, building better futures. *Peace Review*, 33(1), 140–148.

Mitchell, T., Arseneau, C., Thomas, D., & Smith, P. (2019). Towards an Indigenous-informed relational approach to Free, Prior, and Informed Consent (FPIC). *International Indigenous Policy Journal*, 10(4), 1–28.

Mollett, S. (2016). The power to plunder: Rethinking land grabbing in Latin America. *Antipode* 48(2), 412–432.

Motta, S. C., and Nilsen, A. G. (2011). *Social Movements in the Global South: Dispossession, Development, and Resistance*. London: Palgrave.

Navas, G., Mingorria, S., and Aguilar-González, B. (2018). Violence in environmental conflicts: The need for a multidimensional approach. *Sustainability Science*, 13(3), 649–660.

Nixon, R. (2011). *Slow Violence and the Environmentalism of the Poor*. Cambridge, MA: Harvard University Press.

Odeny, B., and Bosurgi, R. (2022). Time to end parachute science. *PLoS Med* 19(9), e1004099.

Ødegaard, C. V., and Rivera Andía, J. J. (2019). *Indigenous Life Projects and Extractivism: Ethnographies from South America*. London: Palgrave Macmillan.

Office of the United Nations High Commissioner for Human Rights (OHCHR). (2015). Belize government's actions show troubling disregard for Maya property rights. www.ohchr.org/en/NewsEvents/Pages/DisplayNews.aspx?NewsID=16208&LangID=E.

Peller, H., Penados, F., and Wainwright, J. (2023). Class processes and agrarian change in southern Belize, 1981–2020. *Journal of Peasant Studies*, 50(7), 2851–2871.

Penados, F. (2019). Indigenous governance and education in Belize: Lessons from the Maya land rights struggle and Indigenous education initiatives. In E. A. McKinely and L. T. Smith, eds., *Handbook of Indigenous Education*. Singapore: Springer Nature, pp. 207–228.

Penados, F., Gahman, L., and Smith, S. J. (2022). Land, race, and (slow) violence: Indigenous resistance to racial capitalism and the coloniality of development in the Caribbean. *Geoforum*, 1(45), 1–11. https://doi.org/10.1016/j.geoforum.2022.07.004.

Penados, F., Gahman, L., Smith, S. J., and Alexander, J. (2021). Responding to the crisis of COVID-19 (and capitalism): Land defence in the face of state-sponsored dispossession and food system shock. *Agrarian South Network Research Bulletin*, 1(9), 15–28.

Quijano, A. (2000). Coloniality of power and Eurocentrism in Latin America. *International Sociology*, 15(2), 215–232.

Rivera Cusicanqui, S., (2020). *Ch'ixinakax utxiwa: On Decolonising Practices and Discourses*. Cambridge: Polity.

Roanhorse, R. (2015). Postcards from the apocalypse. *Uncanny: A Magazine of Science Fiction and Fantasy*, 1(20), 131–136. www.uncannymagazine.com/article/postcards-from-the-apocalypse.

Robinson, C. J. (2020). *Black Marxism: The Making of the Black Radical Tradition* (3rd edition). Chapel Hill: University of North Carolina Press.

Schilling-Vacaflor, A., and Flemmer, R. (2020). Mobilising free, prior and informed consent (FPIC) from below: A typology of indigenous peoples' agency. *International journal on minority and group rights*, 27(2), 291–313.

Schilling-Vacaflor, A., and Eichler, J. (2017). The shady side of consultation and compensation: 'Divide-and-rule' tactics in Bolivia's extraction sector. *Development and Change*, 48(6), 1439–1463.

Shoman, A. (1994). *A History of Belize in Thirteen Chapters*. Belize City: Angelus Press.

Shoman, A. (2018). *Guatemala's Claim to Belize: The Definitive History*. Belize City: Image Factory.

Simpson, A. (2007). On ethnographic refusal: Indigeneity, 'voice', and colonial citizenship. *Junctures*, 9, 67–80.

Simpson, L. B. (2017). *As We Have Always Done: Indigenous Freedom through Radical Resistance*. Minneapolis: University of Minnesota Press.

Smith, L. T. (2012). *Decolonizing Methodologies: Research and Indigenous Peoples*. London: Zed Books.

Smith, S. J., Penados, F., and Gahman, L. (2022). Desire over damage: Epistemological shifts and anticolonial praxis from an Indigenous-led community health project. *Sociology of Health & Illness*, 44, 124–141.

Supreme Court of Belize (SCB). (2007). *Aurelio Cal v. Belize*, Claims No. 171 and 172.

Tallbear, K. (2023). Indigenous genocide and reanimation, settler apocalypse and hope. *Aboriginal Policy Studies*, 10(2), 93–111. https://doi.org/10.5663/aps.v10i2.29.

Thunder Hawk, M. (2007). Native organizing before the non-profit industrial complex, in INCITE: Women of Color against Violence, ed., *The Revolution Will Not Be Funded: Beyond the Non-profit Industrial Complex*. Brooklyn: South End Press, pp. 101–106.

Tomlinson, K. (2019). Indigenous rights and extractive resource projects: Negotiations over the policy and implementation of FPIC. *International Journal of Human Rights*, 23(5), 880–897.

Toledo Anonymous Collective, Gahman, L., Penados, F., and Smith, S. J. (2022). The violence of disavowing Indigenous governance: Exposing the colonial politics of 'development' and FPIC in the Caribbean. *Journal of Political Ecology*, 29(1), 604–617. https://doi.org/10.2458/jpe.5124.

Tran, D., Martinez-Alier, J., Navas, G., and Mingorria, S. (2020). Gendered geographies of violence: A multiple case study analysis of murdered women environmental defenders. *Journal of Political Ecology*, 27(1), 1189–1212.

Tuck, E. (2009). Suspending damage: A letter to communities. *Harvard Educational Review*, 79(3), 409–428.

Tuck, E., and Yang, K. W. (2012). Decolonization is not a metaphor. *Decolonization: Indigeneity, Education, and Society*, 1(1), 1–40.

Tynan, L. (2021). What is relationality? Indigenous knowledges, practices and responsibilities with kin. *cultural geographies*, 28(4), 597–610.

Virtanen, P. K. (2019). Ancestors' times and protection of Amazonian Indigenous biocultural heritage. *AlterNative: An International Journal of Indigenous Peoples*, 15(4), 330–339.

Wainwright, J. (2011). *Decolonizing Development: Colonial Power and the Maya*. London: Wiley-Blackwell.

Wainwright, J. (2021). The Maya and the Belizean state: 1997–2004. *Latin American and Caribbean Ethnic Studies*, 17(3), 320–349. https://doi.org/10.1080/17442222.2021.1935694.

Ward, T. (2011). The right to free, prior, and informed consent: Indigenous peoples' participation rights within international law. *Northwestern University Journal of International Human Rights*, 10, 54–84.

Whyte, K. (2020). Too late for indigenous climate justice: Ecological and relational tipping points. *Wiley Interdisciplinary Reviews: Climate Change*, 11(1), e603.

Wright, C., and Tomaselli, A. (2019). *The Prior Consultation of Indigenous Peoples in Latin America*. Abingdon: Routledge.

Yaffe, N. (2018). Indigenous consent: A self-determination perspective. *Melbourne Journal of International Law*, 19(2), 703–749.

Zapatista Army of National Liberation (EZLN) (2015). *Critical Thought in the Face of the Capitalist Hydra*. Durham: Paperboat Press.

Zeng, Y., Twang, F., and Carrasco, R. (2022). Threats to land and environmental defenders in nature's last strongholds. *Royal Swedish Academy of Sciences*, 51, 269–279.

Acknowledgements

Funding awarded by the University of Liverpool Library's Open Research Team made it possible for this Element to be published open access, making the digital version freely available for anyone to read and reuse under a Creative Commons licence.

Research Ethics Statement

This research was approved by the Central University Research Ethics Committee at the University of Liverpool (Project ID: 5392) and the Campus Research Ethics Committee at The University of the West Indies (Reference: CEC1114/05/19). Participatory co-design and co-authorship with Indigenous Maya communities and activists were critical aspects of the collaboration, hence, Free, Prior and Informed Consent was obtained through appropriate and iterative processes grounded in community protocols, village customs, and principles related to cultural safety and self-determination. Details on the consent process, ethical commitments, and complex politics of conducting research with/for/by Indigenous communities are elaborated in Section 1.

presence in historical sources such as maps and treaties, and in reconnecting Indigenous collections in museums with their source communities. He co-leads the "Green Toolkit for a New Space Economy" project, which aims to widen the space sector's understanding of sustainability to include the cultural and social dimensions. His collaborators include King's Digital Lab at King's College London, The Alan Turing Institute, and Nordamerika Native Museum Zurich. His research interests are on the process of meaning-making, particularly in understanding senses of time and place, and on the repercussions of trauma and disruption. His research on early modern futurity has been published in *Historical Research*, and he teaches courses on cultural astronomy, public history, and digital history.

Advisory Board

Ann McGrath, *Australian National University*

Camilla Brattland, *Arctic University of Norway (UIT)*

Dalo Njera, *Mzuzu University*

Kalpana Giri, *The Regional Community Forestry Training Center for Asia and the Pacific (RECOFTC)*

Simone Athayde, *Florida International University*

Joe Bryan, *University of Colorado Boulder*

Kanyinke Sena, *Egerton University*

Kyle Powys Whyte, *University of Michigan*

Dale Turner, *University of Toronto*

Michael Hathaway, *Simon Fraser University*

Paige West, *Columbia University*

Pratik Chakrabarti, *University of Houston*

Rauna Kuokkanen, *University of Lapland*

Shannon Speed, *University of California Los Angeles*

Mike Dockry, *University of Minnesota*

About the Series

Elements in Indigenous Environmental Research offers state-of-the-art interdisciplinary analyses within the rapidly growing area of Indigenous environmental research. The series investigates how environmental issues and processes relate to Indigenous socio-economic, cultural and political dynamics.

For EU product safety concerns, contact us at Calle de José Abascal, 56–1°, 28003 Madrid, Spain or eugpsr@cambridge.org.